When It Comes to ————
GUYS,
———————What's Normal?

Also by Bernice Kanner

*Pocketbook Power: How to Reach the Hearts and
  Minds of Today's Most Coveted Consumers—Women*

Are You Normal About Sex, Love, and Relationships?

*The Super Bowl of Advertising:
  How the Commercials Won the Game*

Are You Normal About Money?

The Best 100 TV Commercials . . . and Why They Worked

Lies My Parents Told Me

Are You Normal?

When It Comes to
GUYS,
What's Normal?

BERNICE KANNER

ST. MARTIN'S GRIFFIN
NEW YORK

www.stmartins.com

Book design by Ellen Cipriano

Library of Congress Cataloging-in-Publication Data

Kanner, Bernice.
    When it comes to guys, what's normal? / Bernice Kanner.
      p. cm.
    ISBN 0-312-34816-9
    EAN 978-0312-34816-8
      1. Men—United States—Attitudes.   2. Masculinity—United
States.   I. Title.
    HQ1090.3.K36 2005
    305.31—dc22   2005042760

First Edition: June 2005

10 9 8 7 6 5 4 3 2 1

Contents

Foreword   *vii*

1 Who You Are   1

2 In the Ethics Department   8

3 In Sickness and in Health   22

4 Before the Mirror and in the John   35

5 In the Closet   44

6 In Money Matters   55

7 Between the Sheets   63

8 With Family and Friends: Kids, Partners,
   Parents, and Friends   72

9 Behind the Wheel   91

10 On the Job   108

11 In the Manners Department   122

12 In the Kitchen, at the Supermarket,
    In a Restaurant, and Around the Dinner Table   129

13 At Home   144

14 Among Gadgets   149

15 Out of this World (Spiritually Speaking)   160

16 At the Gym: Babying and Buffing Bodies   168

17 Holidays and Vacations   180

18 At Leisure: Men . . . o . . . pause   199

19 With Eccentricities   211

20 Whaddya Know?   227

21 Have You Ever . . . ?   234

Foreword

When it comes to guys, what's "normal"?

How often do men visit the doctor, shop, or shave? How often do they run out of gas on the highway? Who controls the television remote in most households?

The Gillette Company has been committed to understanding men for more than a hundred years, since King C. Gillette was granted patent #775,134 on November 15, 1904, for a revolutionary new product called the safety razor. After years of toying with inventions, King Gillette hit upon the brilliant idea of a razor with a safe, inexpensive, and disposable blade. He knew at once it would fly.

And fly it did.

In the years since Gillette launched the first safety razor, we have pioneered every significant innovation in shaving, from stainless steel blades to twin blades mounted on springs to our most advanced offering yet, the M3Power shaving system. Each of these innovations has been driven by our understanding of men—their behavior, their aspirations, and their demands. Indeed, as men have evolved in their attitudes and beliefs, so too have our products, in keeping with Gillette's time-honored credo: "There is a better way to shave and we will find it."

Well into the twenty-first century, we continue to innovate and to search for a better shave. Searching includes knowing how our customers are changing and catching the subtle nuances in their lives.

When Bernice Kanner presented the idea of a book exploring the habits and idiosyncrasies of guys to us at The Gillette Company, we were intrigued. Her Are You Normal? series of books crackled with startling insights about love, money, romance—many areas of how people behave. When she wanted to put men under the microscope, we jumped at the chance to hold the lens—to undertake original research and to supply her with statistics and information that we have amassed about men over the past century.

We are proud to have been a resource for this unprecedented exploration into guys' behaviors . . . to help you understand "what's normal."

We hope you'll enjoy this fascinating journey.

—Peter Hoffman
President, Blades & Razors
The Gillette Company

When It Comes to ——— GUYS, ——— What's Normal?

1

Who You Are

There are 102.2 million of you (men, 18 and older) in America. Some 19.56 million of you are 25 to 34, just a shade less than the 19.68 million women that age. In a recent year 85 percent of all men held a job, accounting for 53 percent of the workforce. You earned on average a weekly salary of $732 ($164 more than what the average woman earned).

The average American man measures five feet nine inches (about a quarter of an inch taller at night than in the daytime) and weighs 180 pounds. He has a 41-inch chest, a 35-inch waist, and a 40.5-inch hip. His waist and hips will thicken with age and when he gains weight it will most likely be in the center of his body, particularly around his stomach. His penis is six inches long while standing at attention. He is circumcised (some 78 percent of American men are). He'll live to be 73.

Four in 10 expect to make it to 100, but few want to. The average age they want to live to is 91. Four times as many men fear ending up in Shady Acres as they do passing quickly from a sudden disease. Men die from accidents, suicide, cirrhosis of the liver, and homicide at a rate at least twice as high as women do, and they're even more likely than women to die due to floods:

driving around barricades in low-lying flood zones and drowning in high water.

Two out of three feel a lot younger than their chronological years and 63 percent figure they've got more energy than most other guys their age. They also have more confidence. Seventy-six percent feel more self-assured than most of their friends. Only three percent concede that they generally need several attempts to get the car parked.

At age 45 the typical American male has a one in 3,333 chance of developing prostate cancer. By age 75, the chance drops to one in nine. The average American man over 45 has a nine percent chance of dying from lung cancer, a 5.6 percent chance of being taken out by a stroke, a 3.7 percent chance of succumbing to pneumonia, and a 2.8 percent chance of giving it up to diabetes. As he ages, the average guy loses 12 to 20 pounds of muscle, 15 percent of his bone density, and two inches of height. His counts of oxygen-carrying red blood cells also drop along with his sexual vigor and testosterone levels.

The typical man has 100,000 hairs on his head (the diameter of those strands is twice that of women's hair) and he loses 20 to 100 of them a day. By age 50, the typical man has lost 12.1 teeth. If offered a Groundhog Day invitation to return to any age, the mean age men chose is 39.

The typical American man is neither a John Wayne tough guy nor a "New Man" metrosexual. (In fact, only three percent of men consider themselves metrosexuals. Another 16 percent claim to share some characteristics but abhor the label. Thirty-eight percent have never heard the term and 45 percent describe themselves as old-fashioned, dyed-in-the-wool normal.) Rather than embracing "mancipation," rejecting traditional male roles, Mr. Joe Average sees himself as a provider, progenitor, protector. But he spurns the notion that biology is as important as culture in creating masculine and feminine attributes. He accepts the truth to the stereotype that he's a slob. Nonetheless, he's mystified by the avalanche of misandry, hatred of men, he sees in TV commercials.

Men are far more likely to profess that they admire an easy-going regular guy who's honest, dependable, and smart than a money-grubbing power broker. They rank honesty and dependability as the most important fiber in a man's character followed by his willingness to help. Less significant, but by no means unimportant, are a sense of humor and authenticity.

The typical American man laughs 15 times a day and cries 1.4 times a month. While 63 percent of men in their 50s have never seen their father well up, only 44 percent of those 18 to 29 can say the same. Almost 90 percent of men classify themselves as shy.

The average guy spends 7.5 hours a night or 220,000 hours in his life sleeping. Chances are it's in a chilly room and on a firm mattress rather than a soft one with two pillows. (Most of the time, though, he keeps the thermostat at 72 degrees—room temperature.) And if he's getting on in years, he's probably disturbing the peace with his raucous snores. (More than 60 percent of older guys are guilty.) Three out of four accuse their partners of hogging the covers. He has over 1,460 dreams a year.

Almost all American men (84 percent) have graduated from high school but just 28 percent have a college degree. The typical American man with a bachelor's degree makes $66,810. Those with only a high school diploma make an average of $30,414. The typical man's vocabulary consists of 5,000 to 6,000 words.

The typical man has 14.3 sex partners in his life—he has not paid money for any of them. He was 16.2 years old when he lost his virginity and found his sweet spot, and 27.1 when he married. (Fifty-five percent are currently married and 8.3 percent are currently divorced.) Typically he does not admit to having had an outside affair. He enjoys sex 135 times a year (okay, *has* it), releasing 120 million to 600 million sperm into the world with each orgasm. (Only about 400 of them will get anywhere *near* the egg.) Two out of three uncommitted men store condoms within three feet of their beds.

The average guy received his first credit card when he was 25 years and three months old, and bought his first stock, bond, or mutual fund at around age 27. That's two to three years before the average woman does. The typical man who owns a house spent $175,400 to buy it. More than half (53 percent) feel a cut in the capital gains tax would stimulate the economy.

Women may control the purse strings but the typical man still thinks that when it comes to power, it's his world. You know the old Chinese proverb that men have their say but women have their way? They're not buying it. They feel that while women resolve the day-to-day issues, it's men who settle the life-changing disputes. More men say that they decide where the family lives rather than their partner and that they have much more sway in how money is spent. The typical man still identifies with Luca Brasi's sentiment in *The Godfather*: "May your first child be a masculine child."

The average working stiff spends about half as much time as his gender counterpart on taking care of the house and kids. But he spends a lot more time at his job and on enjoying life. The average guy has a tad more than five hours of leisure time a day: he spends over half of it watching TV, 20 minutes at sports, and another 20 minutes relaxing and "thinking." The average guy spends just 50 minutes a day caring for his family and less than 45 minutes on household chores. (In contrast, the average working woman spends an hour and a half and one hour 20 minutes on those tasks respectively.) Only 19 percent of men do housework daily and 34 percent claim they help with meals or cleanup.

Most likely he works full time (88 percent do v. 67 percent of women). The average man has 16 years of work experience and been on the job on average 2,147 hours in the past year: women worked an average of 1,675. His median household income is $42,228. The average guy spends 3.7 hours a week at work doing personal chores online and 5.9 hours a week going online at home for work.

The typical guy is *not* a walk fast, eat on the run, do two things at the same time creature, although if he lives in the

Northeast, he's likelier to be a Type A than if he hails from any-where else in America. Nor is he a happy-go-lucky dude. Only one in five (19 percent) whistles, sings, or hums while he works. Sixty-eight percent consider themselves homebodies, yet only 38 percent call themselves couch potatoes. The typical American male turns the other cheek far more often than he tries to get even. Three out of four tend to forgive others who have com-mitted wrongs against them. The typical American man is not a feminist: only 14 percent say that label applies to them.

Joe Average can read small print better than most women and blinks half as often. And according to anthropologist Helen Fisher, he has 11 percent fewer neurons than women in areas specializing in perceiving different sounds associated with language—meaning he's not as verbally skilled as women and is less sensitive to touch. Alas, he's also far likelier to be color-blind and has a weaker "location memory" than most women. In a memory test, men remembered 70 percent fewer of the items in an office than women did.

The typical man is a proud patriot. Ninety percent believe in supporting their country, right or wrong. Seventy-two percent fly an American flag or display one on their car, and 29 percent look askance at the American Civil Liberties Union. By and large they consider the Marines the branch of the military with the most prestige, followed by the Air Force. The Army edges out the Navy. The least prestigious of the Armed Forces, in their viewpoint: the Coast Guard. Almost all speak English although 23 million (nearly one in five) speak a language other than En-glish at home.

Today, only 31 percent (and 46 percent of women) have left home, finished school, gotten married, had a kid, and become fi-nancially independent by age 30—the traditional benchmarks of adulthood—compared with 65 percent of men and 77 per-cent of women in 1960. The typical American man resides within 50 miles of where he mainly grew up.

Almost three out of four live "en famille." Slightly more than one in 10 live alone. Just a third of those who live alone are "seniors" whereas most women living by themselves are older. Just 13 percent of guys living alone are widowers and 38 percent are divorced or separated. Nearly half of men who live alone (46 percent) have never been married. If Joe Average is divorced, chances are he didn't initiate it. Three out of four times, it's the woman who does.

When he's feeling blue, the typical man might seek solace in the TV (35 percent) or by getting together with friends (33 percent). Twenty-nine percent say they're likely to call someone, 23 percent to work out, and 18 percent to pour themselves a stiff one. Twenty-six percent would likely tackle a household repair or work on the car—roughly the same number who'd likely open the fridge to banish the blues. Fewer than 10 percent are likely to clean, shop, cook, or submerge in a hot bath—recourses women often take. One in five might pray or read. The 38 percent who live with a dog might roughhouse with him: 83 percent profess they *always* pick up Rover's droppings.

Hands down his favorite color is blue, preferably the darker shades between navy and royal. Green comes in second. Purple edges out red a tad but principally if it's called grape. (Purple, once considered feminine, frightens some conservative guys, however.) Red is beloved by economically secure risk-takers. Orange, especially the bright fluorescent shade, has traditionally been men's least liked color.

Two out of five men—38 percent—believe that money buys happiness, but alas, 78 percent feel that contentment is fleeting. Most would not change their lives if given the opportunity to do so. For most, success has nothing to do with the size of their bank account. For 87 percent it's being a great husband and dad and for 85 percent, having a happy marriage or raising successful children.

- ➤ 53 percent have donated blood.
- ➤ 58 percent voted in a recent presidential election.
- ➤ 13 percent have spent a night in jail; 2 percent will go to prison sometime in their life.

- ➤ 26 percent smoke.
- ➤ 24 percent share their household with a tabby.
- ➤ 21 percent have high blood pressure.
- ➤ 64 percent shudder at body piercing other than ears.
- ➤ 41 percent have contributed to a disaster relief fund.
- ➤ 69 percent have at least once worked for a woman boss.
- ➤ 19 percent have been a burglary victim.
- ➤ 40 percent use a credit card at least once a week.
- ➤ 65 percent have disability insurance.
- ➤ 77 percent button their shirt from the top down v. from the bottom up.
- ➤ 43 percent have tried to get out of jury duty.
- ➤ 54 percent will drink straight from the container when no one's around.
- ➤ 30 percent have participated in at least one boycott.
- ➤ 84 percent would give a ball they caught in the stands to their companion.
- ➤ 21 percent usually cross their legs when seated: 45 percent know it's bad for circulation.
- ➤ 62 percent have stood up to a bully even at the risk of physical harm to themselves.
- ➤ 97 percent when offered a new pen to write with will sign their own name.

When It Comes to Guys, What's Normal? takes a look at who men really are, how they behave in the kitchen, bathroom, office, driver's seat, and wherever they happen to be on the planet. So pull up a chair and see how you compare.

2

In the Ethics Department

DO YOU EVER FIB?

Ever? Some 91 percent of us lie regularly. One in five says he can't make it through a single day without conscious, premeditated white lies. Men are more likely than women to fib, and the younger they are, the looser with the truth.

WHEN YOU LIE DO YOU
CONVINCE YOURSELF THAT YOU'RE NOT?

Two studies from the University of Washington have shown that one in ten liars actually believes that he's telling the truth. That makes them somewhat immune to lie detector tests. Guys with a good imagination are likelier to convince themselves that their lies are the truth than women.

THINK MOST PEOPLE ARE HONEST?

While 54 percent of men think most people are honest, 45 percent believe an honest man can't get elected to high office. Twenty-one percent admit they would keep the change if a cashier accidentally gave them too much back.

CONSIDER YOURSELF PART OF
THE COMPENSATION CULTURE?

Just four percent are ready to sue if they trip on a pothole. Twenty-eight percent say they'd be mad, but would recognize it was their own fault. Two out of three are fence-sitters.

HOW DO YOU FEEL ABOUT
MAKING PATERNITY TESTING ROUTINE?

Half of all men favor making paternity testing at childbirth routine, but only 32 percent of women do, according to a University of Washington study. Generally, fewer than one percent of married women bear children other than their husband's. Many women supporters think it's an easy way to reassure their husbands of their faithfulness, and some want to make sure that, for health reasons, their children have correct information about their genetic heritage.

EVER TRIED TO PAD AN INSURANCE BILL
TO COVER YOUR DEDUCTIBLE?

Four in ten guys admit they've fudged a diagnosis or tried to inflate the bill so insurance picks it up.

WOULD YOU REPORT INSURANCE FRAUD OF A FRIEND?

Twenty-nine percent of men—even more in the Northeast—say they'd never report insurance fraud committed by someone they knew. Women are far more likely to blow the whistle. However, men are significantly more inclined to report someone if there is a monetary reward.

EVER NOT LISTED A PREEXISTING CONDITION TO GET A BETTER HEALTH INSURANCE DEAL?

If the insurance company finds out, I'd be left high and dry, say two-thirds of men. A fourth see nothing wrong with it and might very well do so, while another eight percent already have.

EVER TRIED TO PASS OFF MIX OR STORE-BOUGHT AS HOMEMADE?

Some 59 percent of men have fudged a bit here, using a mix to whip up made-from-scratch cakes or cookies or even buying it outright from the store and throwing away the telltale box.

EVER LIED ON A RÉSUMÉ OR JOB APPLICATION?

Eighty-six percent of men say they have fudged something about their education, employment skills, or some other personal information.

PARK IN A SPACE DESIGNATED FOR A HANDICAPPED DRIVER?

If they knew they wouldn't be caught 14 percent of men say they would take advantage of the close-in parking.

HOOK UP CABLE ILLEGALLY?

Again, if they knew they wouldn't be caught, 16 percent of men (v. 11 percent of women) say they would try to watch *The Sopranos* for free. West Coasters are the most likely to do the illegal hookup.

EVER SECRETLY CLIPPED FLOWERS FROM A PARK OR NEIGHBOR'S GARDEN?

Just 17 percent of men admit they've nipped a blossom or two.

WOULD YOU DRIVE THROUGH A TOLLBOOTH WITHOUT PAYING IF YOU KNEW YOU WOULDN'T GET CAUGHT?

Men (12 percent) are more likely than women (7.5 percent) to say they would do so.

WHAT IS YOUR WORST VICE?

Forty-one percent of men say they haven't any: that they're pure as driven snow. But one in six owns up that he hangs out in strip clubs, and another 15 percent read girlie magazines. Two in five (39 percent) fess up to indulging in Internet porn.

WOULD YOU SECRETLY HELP YOUR DAUGHTER GET BIRTH CONTROL?

One in four dads says he would help his daughter get birth control—and hide it from her mother if he suspected mom would resist.

EVER SWITCHED TAGS IN A STORE TO PAY LESS?

One in 10 guys admits to doing that or walking out with merchandise that he didn't pay for.

WOULD YOU USE A CROOKED BROKER IF YOU BENEFITED FROM HIS SHADY DEALS?

Two out of five guys say that as long as what they were doing wasn't strictly illegal they'd stick with the gain.

WOULD YOU LET A FRIEND DRIVE DRUNK?

More than one in every three guys (38 percent) would, and one out of three would even let it happen more than once.

WOULD YOU LEAVE THE SCENE OF A CRIME IF YOU WERE SURE YOU COULD GET AWAY WITH IT?

Ten percent of men say they'd hightail it out of there if they scraped the side of a parked car with no one in it or around and figured no one saw. The rest would either leave their contact information on the damaged car or contact the police.

EVER SNOOP IN YOUR HOST'S MEDICINE CHEST?

Some 39 percent of guys admit that they peek in their host's medicine cabinets when using their john.

EVER BRING YOUR OWN FOOD TO
NOSH ON DURING A MOVIE?

Just under half of men say they have taken their own sweets and snacks to the cinema.

BELIEVE IN AN EYE FOR AN EYE?

Seventy-six percent of men believe in capital punishment. Twenty-one percent are equally convinced that the death penalty is wrong. However, 32 percent would prefer to sentence a murderer to life in prison (sans parole) rather than kill him. And 12 percent suspect a lot of innocent people have been wrongly executed.

EVER FILCH FROM THE OFFICE CUPBOARD?

Sixty percent of men admit they take things from work and half steal towels from a health club. Almost a quarter confess to not always repaying loans and 29 percent shoplift.

EVER UNDERSTATE THE NUMBER OF
PREVIOUS PARTNERS TO A PROSPECT TO
MAKE IT HAPPEN?

Some 47 percent of men (and slightly fewer women) either have or would understate the number of their previous partners in order to convince a new prospect to have sex.

THINK THREE YEARS IN JAIL IS ABOUT RIGHT FOR THROWING A PET DOG INTO ONCOMING TRAFFIC DURING A BOUT OF ROAD RAGE?

One in four men feels the sentence is too harsh, and one in four figures it's too lenient. The rest view it as appropriate.

EVER "BORROWED" SOMETHING FROM A HOTEL ROOM?

That sure looks like a Hilton towel in your bathroom. Twenty-nine percent of men admit packing the hotel towels and eight percent have made off with their bathrobe.

ARE YOU COMFORTABLE BEING ON A JURY THAT RECOMMENDS THE DEATH PENALTY FOR A CONVICTED MURDERER?

Almost three out of five men (58 percent) say they'd be all right with this. Thirty-six percent would like to see more convicted criminals executed while 21 percent would opt for fewer executions. Generally speaking, just eight percent of men think the punishments given to criminals are too harsh while 57 percent think they're too soft.

WOULD YOU BE COMFORTABLE HELPING A TERMINALLY ILL PERSON VOLUNTARILY END HIS LIFE?

Just over half of men—52 percent—say they would have no compunction doing this.

DO YOU BELIEVE PEOPLE SHOULD BE CLONED?

Two-thirds of men oppose the cloning of humans. Thirty-eight percent feel strongly it should be banned.

WOULD YOU CONDONE THE CIA COVERTLY ASSASSINATING SUSPECTED ENEMIES OF THE U.S.?

Two out of three men (67 percent) favor it. Putting aside any physical limitations or age issues, 57 percent of men say they'd be willing to fight and, if need be, die to protect President Bush from an assassin.

CONSIDER DOWNLOADING MUSIC STEALING?

Copyright be damned say 58 percent of men. Eleven percent acknowledge that harsher penalties have made them mend their thieving ways. Seventy-eight percent now won't allow others to download music or video files from their computer.

EVER SAID "I LOVE YOU" WHEN YOU KNEW IT WASN'T TRUE?

Turns out that 44 percent of men have committed this particular fib.

DO YOU REGULARLY GOSSIP?

It is not just a women thing. Six percent of men admit their loose lips have sunk ships and that they regularly take part in gossip sessions.

GET YOUR JOLLIES WITH PORN?

Fourteen percent of men regularly look at porn or go to see strippers. Another 30 percent do so occasionally.

SHOULD TOP EXECS BE PROSECUTED IF THEY KNEW THEIR COMPANY WAS TANKING BUT THEY SOLD STOCK BEFORE TAKING THE NEWS PUBLIC?

Only seven percent of men don't consider that a heinous crime worthy of everything the courts can throw at the offenders.

SHOULD MAJOR LEAGUE BASEBALL PLAYERS BE TESTED FOR STEROIDS?

Another clear majority weighs in here. Ninety-one percent of men believe these highly paid and celebrated athletes should be tested for performance-enhancing drugs.

SHOULD OUR RIGHTS AND FREEDOMS COME WITH LIMITS AND RESPONSIBILITIES?

Just 24 percent of men say the rights and freedoms guaranteed by the Constitution's Bill of Rights should be complete and absolute, with no strings attached. Thirty-five percent believe those rights and freedoms were meant to never change while 62 percent believe they should evolve with the times. Fifty-one percent think the protections in the Bill of Rights should apply only to American citizens.

BELIEVE HAVING A BABY OUTSIDE OF MARRIAGE IS MORALLY ACCEPTABLE?

It's pretty much a toss-up with slightly more men believing it's morally acceptable than repugnant.

OKAY TO CRITICIZE THE PRESIDENT?

Men are slightly less open-minded than women here with 54 percent considering that just as patriotic as voting.

BELIEVE THAT BOOKS THAT CONTAIN "DANGEROUS" IDEAS SHOULD BE BANNED FROM SCHOOL LIBRARIES?

Pew Research Center found 39 percent of men adamant that these incendiary books be banned and another six percent lean in that direction. The remainder feel public school libraries should be allowed to carry any books they want.

THINK THERE'S ANYTHING IMMORAL ABOUT DIVORCE?

One in four men (26 percent) consider divorce contrary to their religious and ethical values.

THINK MARIJUANA SHOULD BE LEGALIZED?

While only one in three men (34 percent) want to legalize the use of marijuana, that number is nearly twice as many as a decade ago. And 72 percent believe that people arrested for possessing small amounts of marijuana should be fined rather than jailed. Forty-three percent of men confess they've smoked pot at least once compared with 27 percent of women.

SNOOPED ON YOUR SWEETIE?

It seems women are more likely to do it than men: one in three females concedes she has spied on her lover, compared to only one in four men. Thirty-four percent of men say they'd never snoop but only one in five women make that claim.

WEIGH THE MORAL IMPLICATIONS OF YOUR INVESTMENTS?

Two out of five of those in the market (38 percent) avoid investing in companies that they consider morally, socially, or environmentally irresponsible, while 35 percent just care about the return. Twenty-seven percent make no effort to find out about the moral fiber of the companies in which they invest. Less than one-fifth of one percent of individuals' mutual funds are held in so-called social funds, the debt or equities of companies regarded as socially responsible.

IF A WAITER UNDERCHARGED YOU, WOULD YOU POINT IT OUT?

Not likely. A survey by ICR Research Group found that 24 percent of diners would not correct a server who undercharged them.

EVER SNUCK INTO A SHOW SO AS TO AVOID BUYING A TICKET?

Nineteen percent have snuck into a theater through the exit door or some other way to avoid paying for a ticket.

IF YOU FOUND A WALLET, WHAT WOULD YOU DO?

Assuming there is both cash and an ID in it, nine percent of men admit they'd keep the cash if the incentive was sufficiently powerful (that is, at least $100) while 13 percent would look the other way for $1000 in a wallet. Younger people (between 18 and 34 years old) are likelier than older ones to keep the dough: 21 percent said they'd take the money and run v. two percent of seniors.

DO YOU CHEAT ON YOUR INCOME TAXES?

Nearly one-third of Americans *admit* they do. Thirty-two percent say they wouldn't report $2,000 in cash they earned for sideline work to the Internal Revenue Service. Rich folks are far more willing to cheat on their taxes than those less well off: 45 percent of guys with household incomes above $50,000 say they'd keep mum about that extra unreported dough compared to 24 percent of those earning less than $15,000 a year. (Wonder why they're rich?)

HAVE A POSITION ON DOCTOR-ASSISTED SUICIDE?

While just 13 percent of men feel suicide is morally acceptable, support for it surges to almost one in two if it is doctor-assisted, meaning the activist is terminally ill and in pain.

CUT INMATE MEALS TO TWO A DAY TO SAVE MONEY?

Three out of four guys resent the idea of Club Fed where prisoners get cable TV and gym time. Two meals a day on the public dole, they say, is plenty.

WOULD YOU COMMIT AN UNTRACEABLE CRIME FOR $10 MILLION?

If they knew they wouldn't get caught, 31 percent of men would go criminal for that kind of loot—almost twice as likely as women to snatch the chance. Lower the booty to $100,000 and eight percent of guys would still do it.

IF YOU UNEXPECTEDLY FOUND ILLEGAL DRUGS, WHAT WOULD YOU DO?

Assuming you were certain they were safe, 48 percent of guys expect they'd party. Twenty-one percent would leave the drugs untouched and avoid any chance of hassling with DEA Agent Smith. Sixteen percent say they'd call the cops and turn the stash in while 15 percent would flush it right down the toilet.

WOULD YOU CROSS A PICKET LINE?

Fifty-five percent of men say no, that workers need to stand united, but 45 percent resent the clout that unions wield.

3

In Sickness and in Health

I n 2005, the average Joe can expect to live for 74 years and four months, shelling out on average $2,267 on health care each year.

DO YOU BELIEVE THAT LAUGHTER IS THE BEST MEDICINE?

Most men say laughter can't hurt but more of them believe in better living through chemistry. Fifty-six percent take some medicine daily.

ARE YOU A HYPOCHONDRIAC?

Sure you've been raised to believe big boys don't cry but on the whole, guys, your upper lip is hardly stiff. While fewer than five percent of men admit they fret about every bump and mole, one in five knows his doctor's phone number by heart. Forty-one percent acknowledge that hearing about a medical condition makes them think that perhaps they've got it.

HOW MUCH PAIN CAN YOU TAKE?

To hear them boast you'd think one in five guys (19 percent) could walk on glass or swallow fire. At the other extreme, seven percent of wimps confess to a pain threshold so low they hyperventilate from a paper cut. Ten percent admit that if they see a doctor's needle coming their way they get all woozy.

WORRIED ABOUT BEING A MEDICAL GUINEA PIG?

Blame it on the Tuskegee syphilis study. That decades-long, government-run research program, in which black men with syphilis were deliberately not told they had the disease and were denied treatment, turned off blacks. But more than half of men overall believe medical researchers might use them as "guinea pigs" without their consent. More than one in four men do not trust their doctor to fully explain research participation to them. Sixty-three percent of black men and 38 percent of whites believe that doctors often prescribe medication as a way of experimenting on people without their knowledge or consent, according to research conducted at the University of North Carolina.

TRY TO WORK OUT YOUR PROBLEMS ON YOUR OWN?

Almost one in three men—29 percent—have gone to a shrink or self-help support group to deal with problems including drug and alcohol abuse, weight loss, and mental health and grief support groups. More than four out of five have turned to the Internet, *Physicians' Desk Reference*, or other research tool to learn about a condition.

What's Bothering You?

> ➤ In a year, half experience stomach, muscle, or joint ache.
> ➤ Almost 20 percent are allergic to mold, spores, pollen, or food.
> ➤ Four out of five have bunions, hammertoes, calluses, or other foot faults. That includes 46 percent who've been bedeviled by the athlete's foot fungus. One in four of all men have flat feet and 15 percent have a high arch. Forty-two percent think having their feet hurt is normal.
> ➤ At one time or another, two out of three have had hemorrhoids.
> ➤ 58 percent have occasional sleep disorder.
> ➤ 16 percent have some symptoms of restless leg syndrome.
> ➤ 44 percent have broken a bone. (The most frequent fractured one is the metatarsal in the foot.)
> ➤ 22 percent have gotten sick from food poisoning.
> ➤ Half have pulled their Achilles tendon, that great anatomical cable that functions as a shock absorber to the foot.
> ➤ Three in five experience at least occasional heartburn.

GOT GAD?

The acronym for Generalized Anxiety Disorder, or a dustbin di-agnosis for free-floating anxiety, takes its place alongside panic disorder, obsessive compulsive disorder, phobias (such as fear of spiders, agoraphobia, and social phobia), and post-traumatic stress disorder as the fifth full-blown anxiety disorder. An esti-mated six percent of men suffer from it.

DEPRESSED?

Although twice as many women as men say they're depressed, more than six million American men—one in every 14—suffer from the blahs. Twelve percent have sought treatment for it at one time in their lives. Many don't recognize what's wrong. Rather than becoming sad, most depressed men get irritable or very tired. They feel dead inside, worthless, hopeless, and helpless. Men in their 20s and 70s are most vulnerable to depression as are men who are single, urban, poorly educated, and with lower income.

HOW MANY COLDS DO YOU CATCH IN A "NORMAL" YEAR?

Boys get more colds than girls do but women get them more often than men do. The "normal" guy gets slightly more than one cold a year and most of them begin on Monday. (They're actually "caught" two or three days previously by touching the hand of someone infected.) The average worker calls in less than four sick days a year, with Southerners, Westerners, a poor folk, and those nearing retirement or seeking a job change taking off the most.

GOT AN ACHING BACK?

Fifty-six percent of men have at one time or another been immobilized by back pain. Exercise and sports-related injuries are the likeliest causes, specifically weight lifting followed by golf, basketball, and football. (For women it's running and tennis.)

GETTING ENOUGH FIBER?

Fiber-rich foods help men prevent gastrointestinal diseases, like colon cancer and diverticulitis, but the average guy eats only about half the recommended amount.

HOW OFTEN IN THE PAST YEAR HAVE YOU VOMITED?

While women heave it up on average five times in a given year, men let loose only 1.4 times on average. More men than women never vomit.

DO YOU TELL YOUR DOCTOR EVERYTHING YOU'RE TAKING?

Thirty-eight percent of men play their cards close to their vest, so to speak. And while 70 percent of women claim to tell their doctors all, just 53 percent of men come completely clean.

QUIVER WHEN YOU HEAR "THE DOCTOR WILL SEE YOU NOW"?

Eleven percent of men are afraid to go to the doctor, an anxiety shared by eight percent of women. A third of men will not seek medical help even when experiencing life-threatening symptoms. One in six would ignore chest pain. Fewer than one in three has had a cancer screening in the past year, versus 55 percent of women. While many men still have to be begged and badgered to go for tests, in a recent year more than two out of three of them made their own appointments.

DO YOU GO TO THE DENTIST TWICE A YEAR?

Fewer than one in every 10 guys does, but the advice is more marketing driven than necessity. It originally came from an old toothpaste ad and had no science behind it . . . just like the magic marketing word in shampoo: "repeat"—which doubled sales.

WHAT DO YOU DO WHEN LYING IN THE CHAIR WAITING?

One in three uses the time to catch some zzzs, one in three doodles with the equipment, and one in three tries to calm himself.

HOW DO YOU USUALLY GET RID OF HICCUPS?

Most guys hold their breath while a goodly number resort to a combination of strategies. One in 10 gulps liquid down, seven percent drink while holding their nose, and another seven percent eat sugar. Eight percent claim they never have to deal with the situation as they're never afflicted with hiccups.

DO YOU MONITOR YOUR BLOOD PRESSURE?

More guys don't than do (45 to 40 percent). Another 15 percent used to do it but have abandoned the task. The normal guy's systolic pressure (when the heart contracts) should be lower than 140 millimeters and his diastolic pressure (when the heart relaxes between beats) should come in under 90.

DO A TESTICLE SELF-EXAM ONCE A MONTH?

While the only way testicular cancer is diagnosed is through a self-exam, fewer than half of men regularly inspect themselves in the shower, or anywhere else for that matter.

KEEP ORGANIZED HEALTH AND MEDICAL RECORDS?

Just 38 percent of men keep a medical file with the results of their tests and details about prescriptions, vaccinations, treatments, allergies et al. Thirteen percent keep electronic records.

WHAT'S IN YOUR MEDICINE CABINET?

Twenty-three percent of men stock more than 10 drugs there. Another 37 percent keep five to 10 different prescriptions on hand. Most men dispose of medications when they notice they've expired, but 63 percent figure they have at least one expired medication taking up space. One in five has popped pills past their prime and 17 percent never check expiration dates. On any given day, 45 percent of American men take at least one prescription drug.

BUY DRUGS ONLINE?

For all the talk about finding cheaper prescription drugs, only four percent of men have bought drugs on the Web. Sixty-two percent think it's too risky. Almost half (48 percent) feel comfortable with generics while 16 percent insist on a brand name drug. For the rest, what they bring home from the pharmacy often depends on the price differential, and who is paying, of course.

HOW ABOUT LOOK THEM UP ONLINE?

Men may not be inclined to buy prescriptions online but they're not at all reluctant to look them up there. Thirty-four percent have researched specific drugs, and 28 percent, alternative treatments or medicines. Sixty-three percent have looked up a specific disease or medical problem, and 47 percent, a certain medical treatment or procedure.

ARE YOU ALLERGIC TO PENICILLIN? BEE STINGS?

Hold the penicillin, say 16 percent of men. Another 15 percent have no idea if they're allergic. Eight percent know that bee stings could cause them more than a slight unpleasantness and another 22 percent fret that they might be allergic.

EVER HAD A CONCUSSION?
HOW ABOUT A ROOT CANAL?

Twenty-four percent of men have been concussed and 30 percent have undergone the ultimate dental damper.

DO YOU KNOW YOUR BLOOD TYPE?
YOUR CHOLESTEROL BLOOD LEVEL?

Fifty-four percent of men know their blood type. Only a third of men know their cholesterol level, even though 60 percent have had it checked during the past year.

USUALLY FINISH YOUR PRESCRIPTIONS?

Only half of drug takers always finish the prescribed medication. Sixty percent often try an over-the-counter drug before resorting to a regulated prescription.

REPLACE YOUR DISPOSABLE
CONTACTS EVERY TWO WEEKS?

More than four out of every five men who wear contacts put in new ones in the recommended time frame.

DO YOU SCRATCH MOSQUITO BITES?

Sure you know that scratching releases histamine from the bite, which in turn causes more itching. Still, three out of four men say they can't resist the urge.

A SURGEON YOU KNEW OR
A HIGHLY RATED UNKNOWN: CHOOSE.

More guys (50 percent) would opt for the surgeon they knew, even if he wasn't highly touted, over a stranger with a lot of pedigree (38 percent). Likewise, men are likelier to pick a hospital they know over one that is rated higher.

NEED SOMETHING TO WASH A PILL DOWN?

Only one in seven Americans takes a pill "like a man," that is, without water or other liquid to get it down. Yet, 27 percent of men admit that they have trouble swallowing pills.

DO YOU USE SUNSCREEN?

Just 45 percent of adults overall apply it regularly with a far lesser percent of men lathering on the stuff. Men don't like the "goop factor."

WOULD YOU AVOID USING A
SICK COWORKER'S PHONE?

Three out of four guys would get creative figuring out ways to avoid using an ill colleague's office phone.

ARE YOU A MIGRAINEUR?

Approximately one in every 15 men suffers from migraine—that severe, throbbing pain usually on one side of the head that usually lasts from a few hours to several days.

WOULD YOU EAT LESS TO BE
GUARANTEED TO LIVE LONGER?

Bring on the repast. Seventy percent of men spurn this bargain. For that matter, only 40 percent of men have any interest in reaching really old age.

DO YOU TAKE VITAMIN
OR MINERAL SUPPLEMENTS?

More than half of men do. The most popular are multivitamins; two-thirds of men take them. Vitamin C is also big: nearly 43 percent of men pop that at least occasionally while

34 percent sometimes take Vitamin E. Two out of three men find it a real challenge figuring out which dietary supplements to take.

EVER HAD A COLORECTAL EXAM?

Men are missing out here. Just 43 percent have had the colon cancer screening. Still, that's better than women, of whom only 33 percent have been tested.

HAD A BLOOD PRESSURE TEST RECENTLY?

Sixty-nine percent of men get their blood pressure read at least once a year, and 43 percent have a complete physical examination annually.

HAD A PSA?

Twenty-three percent of all men and 55 percent of those over 55 have had a prostate specific antigen test within the past year. One in six will get the wretched diagnosis of prostate cancer with African-American men likelier to hear the sobering news than the general population.

TESTED FOR BREAST CANCER?

Not likely. Most men think that because they don't have breasts, they're not at risk of getting breast cancer. Wrong. Some 1,500 men get the disease each year: 400 of them die from it.

HOW DO YOU APPLY A BAND-AID?

The overwhelming majority of men remove the paper first before applying the pad. But close to a third use part of the adhesive strip to cover the wound while applying it. Two percent rarely use Band-Aids; they just let it bleed.

WHAT DISEASE FRIGHTENS YOU MOST?

Cancer (especially prostrate and then lung, skin, and colon/rectal) gives more men the willies than anything else followed by HIV/AIDS and then heart disease. Just 13 percent of men are afraid of losing their hair.

HAUNTED BY AIDS?

One in every five men (21 percent) has avoided elective surgery that requires a blood transfusion for fear of contracting the AIDS virus. Eleven percent have cut off contact with people they suspect have it. Thirteen percent have been tested for it.

THINK IF YOU HAD A VASECTOMY YOU MIGHT CHANGE YOUR MIND LATER?

One in 10 guys who goes through this procedure reverses his decision later. The likeliest reason: remarriage.

EVER PRETENDED SICKNESS TO AVOID DOING SOMETHING DULL?

Some 36 percent of men have pretended to suddenly take ill to get out of doing something boring or bothersome.

BEEN TO AN ACUPUNCTURIST LATELY?
OTHER ALTERNATIVES?

In a recent year, six percent of men swallowed their aversion to needles. Altogether, 12 percent have taken an alternative medicine treatment. Fifteen percent have used aromatherapy and 28 percent have used herbal remedies. Nineteen percent regularly take herbal supplements like ginseng, echinacea, and Saint-John's-wort, and five percent have gone to a hypnotist. Forty-four percent have experimented with faith healing, and a third have gone to a chiropractor or masseuse. Five percent have dabbled in reflexology and 12 percent practiced deep-breathing exercises.

WHAT HAPPENS WHEN SHE GETS REALLY SICK?

The stereotype of the husband paralyzed by fear and uncertainty came into being because men despair at being copatients. They're disturbed by their own inability to protect their lover, and most want to bury their heads and hide from what's happening.

4

Before the Mirror and in the John

HOW MUCH TIME DO YOU SPEND PRIMPING?

It's no longer feet hit the floorboards and out the door. Although 27 percent of men say they're on their way within 15 minutes, the average guy spends 24 minutes a day grooming himself and 63 percent take about a half hour to get ready. One in ten take an hour or more. Middle-aged guys spend the most time; older men, the least amount of time.

WHAT WOULD YOU CHANGE ABOUT YOURSELF . . . ONE THING?

If men could change one thing about themselves, most would drop some pounds. More than half want to change their tonnage. Eleven percent of men would sacrifice more than five years of their life to be at their ideal weight. One in three smoke cigarettes as a way to suppress their appetite.

WORRY THAT YOUR JEANS MAKE YOUR BUTT LOOK FAT?

Apparently most guys do, or at least that's what the companies that make jeans believe. They're putting their money where that thought is, scrambling to come out with low-rise cuts, stretchy fabrics, and other "figure-enhancing" styles as a follow-up to Queer Eye for the Straight Guy. Yet "premium" jeans still account for just one percent of the $5 billion U.S. men's denim market.

GOT FACIAL HAIR?

Almost half of all men (46 percent) have none. Twelve percent have stubble, 21 percent sport a goatee, and 22 percent, a mustache. Five percent, have a chinstrap, and two percent, a full beard. Six percent display large sideburns, and three percent, a soul patch. More men actually prefer goatees (31 percent) than wear them.

HOW DO YOU DEAL WITH IT?

More than 90 percent of American men shave. Most begin sometime between their 14th and 15th birthday. Seventy-two percent wield a razor and blade on the 7,000 to 15,000 whiskers that sprout on their face (the same number of hairs as on women's legs and underarms combined), growing 5.5 inches a year (or 26.5 feet in an average lifetime).

HOW OFTEN DO YOU SHAVE?

Men shave on average 24 times a month—780 hours in a life-time, going through 30 blades a year. Forty-four percent shave daily, and 34 percent, every other day. Whereas women see shaving as a chore, most men see it as a skill. What do men think about most when shaving? Three out of five muse about what's on call in the day ahead. Six percent ponder their next romantic encounter and nine percent admire how handsome they are.

WHAT TIME DOES YOUR "FIVE O'CLOCK" SHADOW SURFACE?

How it became known as the five o'clock shadow is as mysterious as the seven-year itch (most marriages that dissolve do so after four years). Fewer than one in five men notice their facial shadow around 5:00 P.M. and 16 percent sense it before then. But almost a third of men don't see it until the morning after and two percent never see one.

ARE YOU FLAKY?

At some point in their life, more than half of men have dandruff. It's especially prevalent when they're stressed, and more likely to occur in winter and fall than in the warmer seasons. Although it's fairly benign, 21 percent of men say they'd rather suffer a headache than dandruff and 17 percent would rather be afflicted by heartburn. One in 10 would rather have an allergic reaction than flecks on their shoulders and nine percent would gladly swap it for athlete's foot. Janssen Pharmaceutica found that one in three dandruff sufferers chose clothing to conceal or downplay their condition.

HOW OFTEN DO YOU GET SHEARED?

Eighteen percent of men get their hair cut every two weeks or more often, with Southerners, the barber's best customers. Fifty-six percent go approximately once a month. More men prefer the neighborhood barber to a stylist (39 percent). Two in five let whoever is behind the chair clip away while 34 percent of men only let their regular stylist/headman tend to their locks. One in five either does it himself or lets someone close to him do it.

HOW OFTEN DO YOU CHECK YOUR HAIR?

Just nine percent of guys deny ever checking their mane. Five percent of self-conscious or self-delighted fellows own up to checking their locks at least 10 times a day. Twelve percent of men try to keep up with the latest hairstyles.

HOW DEPRESSED ARE YOU ABOUT LOSING YOUR HAIR?

Almost half of all men begin balding by age 35. By age 80, almost all pates are bare. Guys with full heads of hair are the ones most worried about losing it. But only 23 percent of guys whose hair was actually thinning were traumatized.

WOULD YOU CONCEAL YOUR BALDING HEAD UNDER A CAP?

While most balding guys do nothing as their shiny scalps emerge, four in 10 try to hide the follicular migration with a cap. One in five resort to some variation of the ear-to-ear three-strand sweep. Hair transplants and Rogaine are slightly more popular than head shaving and toupees. Thirty-six percent of men losing their hair grow some elsewhere in a beard or mustache.

USE HAIR COLOR?

Compelled by both the bedroom and the boardroom, one in 12 American men today colors his hair. NFO Research found sales of hair color for men topped more than $100 million in 2003, triple the amount a decade earlier.

BELIEVE IN THE TOOTH FAIRY?

Call her Teethabell: one in 10 men has had his whitened or bonded or have had some other cosmetic dental work done.

GOT A HAIRY BACK?

Around one in every nine men has this problem and it's a doozy. *New Woman* magazine found that 74 percent of women are sufficiently repulsed by this to turn their own back on these guys. Sensing this opprobrium, eight percent of men have shaved their back.

SHAVE OFF ANY OTHER BODY HAIR?

Surprisingly, 93 percent of men do. Twenty-one percent shape or mold their pubic hair and 16 percent take a razor to their chest. Ten percent have shaved their underarms.

WHICH IS A BIGGER TURNOFF, NOSE HAIR OR A UNIBROW?

Grab the grooming tools. Tufts coming out of noses or ears disgust more people than those who are repulsed by a unibrow or even dirty fingernails. Less off-putting (but still real downers) are long toenails and unkempt beards. Seven out of every 10 men trim their nose hair while another 13 percent say it never grows.

HAVE YOU EVER PLUCKED OR WAXED YOUR EYEBROWS?

Two out of three men (67 percent) raise an eyebrow to that, but 15 percent have done so and another 18 percent have thought about changing their brows.

WHICH COSMETIC PROCEDURES WOULD YOU TAKE FOR FREE?

For 63 percent of men cost is not an issue; they wouldn't go under the knife for vanity's sake, period. For those who would undergo cosmetic surgery, liposuction would attract the most applicants. Nine percent of men say they'd consider having their fat vacuumed away. The second most popular nip and tuck for men: blepharoplasty or eyelid surgery, followed by nose reshaping and gynecomastia, or breast reduction. There are few takers lining up for calf or chin implants or for Botox. One in five plastic surgery patients is male.

DOING ANYTHING TO SAVE FACE?

Twelve percent of guys use a special facial soap. Seven percent use a facial scrub; three percent, an astringent; and one percent, a mask. Twenty-two percent usually slather sunscreen on their face when they're soaking up the rays. Eight percent of men have already had a chemical peel or skin resurfacing or would like to do it.

HOW ABOUT TO SAVE YOUR SKIN?

More than half of men (52 percent) have a problem with their skin and 55 percent buy supplies (they're never called "products") to take care of it. (Marketers have discovered that men respond to words like "supplies" instead of products, and "scruffing" instead of "clarifying" lotions.) Seventeen percent regularly experience razor bumps, and 12 percent each, rough skin, blackheads or whiteheads, and oily skin.

What Else You Got, Whatcha Do, and Whatcha Buying?

According to Strategic Retail, a marketing and retail consulting firm in New York: 73 percent of men purchase hair care products; 13 percent use hairspray; and another 13 percent, hair mousse, spritz, or gel.

- ➤ 61 percent use conditioner.
- ➤ 59 percent wear cologne; 32 percent dab some on daily, but surprisingly, that's down from what it was a few years ago.
- ➤ 74 percent use deodorant.
- ➤ 44 percent soothe on aftershave.

- ➤ 25 percent apply hand and body moisturizer.
- ➤ 28 percent apply lip balm.
- ➤ 6 percent of self-defined straight rural men use nail polish.
- ➤ 22 percent claim to brush after every meal.
- ➤ 6 percent use bronzers or foundation.
- ➤ 9 percent want to have unwanted body hair removed with a laser or by electrolysis.
- ➤ 34 percent would like lazar eye surgery—or have already done it.
- ➤ 11 percent of men have already had a hair transplant or would like to do it.
- ➤ 13 percent have their ears pierced, most commonly with one hole per ear.
- ➤ 14 percent have a tattoo or body piercing.
- ➤ 61 percent have belly button lint with older, hairier guys and those with innie belly buttons the most likely to sport it. 42 percent clean their belly button every day.
- ➤ 63 percent shower in the morning.
- ➤ Most prefer a comb instead of a hairbrush.
- ➤ Slightly less than half brush their teeth up and down.

EVER LET THEM SEE YOU SWEAT?

The average guy *is* sweating it, shedding 200 mg of perspiration from his underarms in one hour at room temperature, 600 mg at a toasty 100 degrees, and 700 mg when emotionally stressed. But you may not be able to tell: 91 percent of them use a deodorant.

EVER HAD A MANICURE?

If he's had one at all, the average guy has gotten it once in his lifetime: right before his wedding. Most often he scrubs at home with a nailbrush and soap. Just four percent of men get manicures regularly.

HOW DO YOU FEEL ABOUT LIPSTICK?

Great on her, not on him. Three out of four men (76 percent) prefer scarlet lips to softer shades of pink. They're evenly divided on favoring matte or glossy lips. Three out of four would find a lipstick message on the bathroom mirror romantic, and 54 percent would consider a little lipstick smeared on their collars the sign of a good date.

HOW WOULD YOU GO ABOUT
WASHING THAT WOMAN OUT OF YOUR HAIR?

Probably he'd tackle it in the shower. A measly four percent of men wash their hair in the bath and one in 10 do it at the sink. Most likely he washes his hair at the beginning of his shower and most likely pouring the shampoo into his hands first rather than dumping it directly on his head. The average man's shower lasts 10.4 minutes.

5

In the Closet

DO CLOTHES MAKE THE MAN?

While most men recognize how superficial that sounds, and liken it to judging a book by its cover, more than four out of five feel that to some extent what they wear reflects who they are.

CONSIDER YOURSELF A FASHION PLATE?

While not exactly on the front ropes of fashion, 87 percent of men would not be subjected to a visit from the fashion police. Fifty-five percent say they're happy with their sense of style and think they're sufficiently dapper.

JUDGE A GUY BY HIS SHOES?

Holes and talking soles deal the prospect out. Shallow as it sounds, one in five men say the person they're meeting gets no further with them if they don't pass the shoe test.

WHAT'S IN YOUR CUPBOARD?

T-shirts are the most common article of clothing in men's wardrobes (more than nine out of 10 guys have them), followed closely by blue jeans. Three out of four men own at least one button-down shirt and two out of three have a sport coat or blazer. Slightly more than half (56 percent) have a business suit hanging in their closet but only 12 percent wear it regularly. Most guys think they look best in jeans.

WHAT SIZE T-SHIRT?

There are more extra large T-shirts crumpled in men's drawers than there are extra small, small, and medium combined. Twenty-seven percent of men take a large, and 15 percent an extra extra large size.

HOW ABOUT A TUX?

Only 16 percent of men own a dinner jacket. Fewer than four percent own a cumberbund. While more than four in every five guys understand what "black tie" indicates on an invitation, half are thrown by the increasingly common "business elegant" or "casual dressy" directives.

CAN YOU TIE A BOW TIE?

Would you believe that it's women, more than men, who know how to tie a bow tie, and that more than half of men haven't mastered it? No mystery why clip-on or preknotted elastic ties were invented.

THINK PINK?

Despite the best efforts of fashion experts to get men to get in touch with their feminine side, 93 percent say they're not inclined to add pink to their wardrobes.

HOW MUCH TIME DO YOU SPEND PICKING OUT WHAT TO WEAR?

Sears spent considerably more time finding out than men spend picking out. Twelve percent say that they spend literally "no time," and one out of four take less than a minute to make their wardrobe selection. Very few take two minutes or more deciding what to wear.

WHERE DOES YOUR WALLET GO?

More than one in four guys don't bother carrying one. Of those who do, three out of four times they stick it in a back pocket rather than in a front one.

DO YOU CLOTHES SHOP FOR PLEASURE?

Almost everyone suspected it and it's true—most men shop only when they need something. While women may find shopping to be emotionally fulfilling, most guys find it purely functional. Only 42 percent admit they make impulse purchases and a negligible number later regret it.

GOT MANDALS?

Some 9.7 million men got into the Spartacus mode in a recent year buying sandals to display their ventilated toes.

EVER WEAR FRENCH CUFFS?

American men don't like the French—including their cuffs. Sixty-three percent of men don't wear them and don't like them. Just 11 percent both like them and wear them.

CONSIDER STRETCH CLOTHES A STRETCH?

A decade ago, men wanted no part of the spandex look, which they associated with John Travolta's peacockery in *Saturday Night Fever*. But instead of cringing, today men are buying. Stretch fibers (now, thanks to technology without the rubbery retractable "boing") are in as much as 15 percent of men's clothing and they're bought by those who want to show off their buff and regular Joes who've no clue why they're so comfortable: the word "stretch" rarely appears on a hangtag.

EVER TRIED ON A BRA?

Some 13 percent of men have admitted trying one on, mostly for fancy dress or a dare, but some for curiosity or pleasure. Most say they found it uncomfortable.

WHAT DO YOU USUALLY WEAR TO WORK?

Only 14 percent of guys wear so-called professional dress to work. Thirty-six percent usually go to the office in business casual and 14 percent in very casual clothing, including jeans, T-shirts, and sandals. A third wear a combination of business casual and professional.

WHAT'S BEEN THE GREATEST CAUSE OF ANY SARTORIAL UNDOING?

Split seams can be a bummer but 62 percent of men claim that at one time or another they have been undone by an undone zipper.

ENJOY LOOKING THROUGH FASHION MAGAZINES?

For 19 percent of men flipping through the styles is fun. That's considerable but nowhere near the 59 percent of women who fancy this. At the same time, 77 percent of men say that what's "in" has no bearing on what he puts on.

GOT A JEWELRY STASH?

Not likely. Most men have an old set of cuff links, a few tiepins, a watch, and if they're married, their wedding ring. Three out of four married men wear their band.

WHERE DO YOU WEAR YOUR WATCH?

Most guys wear their watch on their left wrist, regardless of whether they're right-or left-handed. Fewer than two in every 100 don't wear a watch. Even though most people own 3.5 watches, they tend to wear the same one daily. And most have them set five minutes ahead of real time.

AVOID WEARING WHITE AFTER LABOR DAY?

While more women cling to this old-fashioned rule, 66 percent of men put away their summer whites when autumn arrives.

WHAT'S THE MOST COMFORTABLE THING TO WEAR?

Both men and women agree jeans are like a second skin (58 percent and 43 percent, respectively) and sweats (17 percent and 25 percent, respectively) are also comfy. From here on the genders divide. Women like to hang around in "PJs" while men prefer wearing nothing or suits!!!

DO YOU WEAR SOCKS?

Seventy-seven percent of men normally wear socks and most of those wear the most unobtrusive they can find. One in five goes almost exclusively with a mid-calf length while 12 percent prefer socks that come just above their ankles. Eight percent like tube socks.

STORE THEM ROLLED OR FLAT?

Rolled wins by a shade: 51 percent prefer them rolled. While socks should match your pants to create a nice vertical line and take undue focus from the ankle, a small percentage of men usually match their socks to their shoes.

BRIEFS OR BOXERS?

Forty-two percent of men prefer briefs and 36 percent, boxers. Just three percent prefer bikinis. Marketers must feel men are obsessed with underwear, because otherwise why would there be so many choices including "action bikinis" and "athletic strings," shorts with breathable mesh pouches and waistband condom pockets, and thongs with "sling support." One new brand promises to "lift, project forward, and improve the wearer's profile." According to Freshpair.com, an online retailer of undergarments, married men change their underwear twice as often as single guys.

DO YOU USE THE VERTICAL SLIT IN YOUR UNDERWEAR?

Some 85 percent of men have discovered another way to pee. They go over.

OWN A JOCKSTRAP?

Eighty-seven percent of men do. Nineteen percent of them own just one and 13 percent, two. Regular is the most popular variety but 17 percent own a cup jock and 15 percent a swimmer.

One in 10 own a wide band and eight percent, a thong-style jock. Most guys bought their jock straps at a sporting goods store. Ten percent found the process embarrassing.

DO YOUR CLOTHES FACE IN ONE DIRECTION IN THE CLOSET?

Just one in four men makes absolutely no effort to have their clothes face in a certain direction. Of those who are more orderly, many more have the hangers point in instead of the open part facing out.

UNTIE AND RETIE YOUR SHOES EACH TIME YOU PUT THEM ON?

Astonishingly, most men do. Still one in four casually slips on his shoes without untying and retying them. Or else, they favor Velcro, slip-ons, or the untied look.

WHICH SHOE DO YOU USUALLY PUT ON FIRST?

It's pretty much a toss-up with the right shoe edging out the left as primo footwear by a narrow margin. Almost three out of four left-handed people, however, slip on their left foot first.

USE SHOE TREES?

Although the average foot perspires a pint of moisture a day—sweat that stays in the lining deteriorating the shoe and stinking up the place—fewer than one in five men regularly installs cedar trees into his footwear to hold their shape.

WHAT DO YOU WEAR TO BED?

Sixteen percent don't wear a stitch. Twenty-four percent slip into pajamas and 31 percent head to bed in their underwear. One in 10 sleeps in a T-shirt or undershirt and seven percent, in sweatpants.

EVER WASH A GARMENT WITH A DRY CLEAN ONLY LABEL?

Nearly half of men have laundered something that warned against it.

EVER BEEN REALLY CREATIVE TO COVER A STAIN?

Twelve percent of folks have turned their clothes inside out to avoid doing laundry.

DRY-CLEAN YOUR SUITS AND COATS AT THE END OF THE SEASON?

Although some invisible food stains can oxidize and turn brown when allowed to hibernate, fewer than half of all men routinely schlep their garments to the dry cleaner seasonally.

KNOW HOW TO PROPERLY MEASURE A COAT THAT FITS WELL?

Most men rely on a tagged size without considering the manufacturer's vagaries. Most know their chest measurement, although more than half think that a size 42 jacket means a

42-inch chest. (It doesn't: most manufacturers cut the chest of the jacket four inches larger than the actual chest measurement of the individual. So a size 42 jacket would have an actual chest [outseam] measurement of 46.)

EVER WEAR DIRTY UNDERWEAR WHEN THERE'S NOTHING CLEAN?

One in five men (and eight percent of women) sometimes raids the laundry basket and one in three would wear a stained shirt to work if he had no meetings planned.

BOUGHT DESIGNER DUDS?

Almost half of all men have bought an item of designer clothing in the past year—even more than the percent of women who have done so, according to Mintel.

WHAT WOULD YOU WANT TO BE BURIED IN?

Most guys are too into living to worry about what they'll be wearing when it's all over. Half of those who will be buried (instead of cremated) expect to spend eternity in a suit (with or without a tie). The rest prefer to go out in casual comfort. Eighteen percent wonder why they should care: they want a closed coffin so you can skip the duds altogether.

SHOP FOR CLOTHES BY YOURSELF?

Used to be the ladies bought most of what men wore. But by 2003, according to NPD Group, men had become far more self-selecting and self-sufficient. More than 45 percent of men's

clothing sold last year was bought by men shopping unaccompa-
nied by a woman. STS Market Research says guys bought 69
percent of their jeans, slacks, shorts, shirts, sweaters, and other
casual wear. Almost one in every five women bought underwear
or socks for their men in the past year. Men shop less frequently
than women, but buy considerably more each visit. While they
love bargains, they love service even more and willingly spend
the extra $ for that extra TLC.

HOW ABOUT BUY HER CLOTHES?

Most haven't even a clue what size she wears. According to
MRI, 16 percent of men have purchased some item of women's
clothing in the past year with married and engaged men the likeliest to do so. Would you believe bras and underpants are among
the most common stuff they buy? In a recent year, six percent of
men bought a dress for their lady.

6

In Money Matters

WHAT'S IN YOUR WALLET:
HOW OFTEN DO YOU CHECK?

The mean amount toted around is $104 and change. Ten percent of guys rarely if ever count what they're carrying around while 15 percent do a daily tally. The rest check their stash when they're going to the bank to see if they need to withdraw cash or when they're in a store to see if they've got enough to buy something.

IS YOUR DOUGH ORGANIZED?

Not for the one in five guys who throws his money loose in his pockets. For men with wallets, 72 percent stow their bills in progressive order and 52 percent save old pennies. One in five has had his pocket picked or wallet stolen. Forty-seven percent squirrel spare bills around the house for emergencies. Just 46 percent keep their money and credit cards separate.

HOW MANY CREDIT CARDS ARE YOU CARRYING AROUND?

The average guy has eight to 10 credit cards in his pocket, including three to four bank cards. Twenty-three percent have at least one debit card. Men carry an average of $3,932 in credit-card debt, $1,348 more than the average $2,584 debt for women. Fifty-one percent of guys don't always pay their balance in full—thus generating avoidable (and wickedly steep) interest charges.

HOW LONG DO YOU KEEP A CREDIT CARD?

Some 26 percent of men have held theirs for a decade or longer; 11 percent have had the same card for seven to nine years. One in four obviously "churn": they've had their prime card for only one to three years.

GOT A FAVORITE—"HEADS" OR "TAILS"?

Chances are it is heads. Guys are three times likelier to call heads than they are to call tails. Likewise, in spinning a racket for tennis they're three times likelier to call up than down.

ARE YOU MORE LIKELY TO SELL STOCKS THAT HAVE GONE UP OR UNLOAD THOSE THAT HAVE TANKED?

Three out of four are likelier to cash in the winners. In fact, 40 percent admit they often throw good money after bad, spending big time, say, to fix a jalopy just because they've already spent a lot on it. Or they'll hold a pig stock because they don't want to admit to themselves that they've picked a porker.

SHOULD CHILDREN INHERIT EQUALLY,
NO MATTER WHAT?

Two-thirds of dads (64 percent) say that no matter how much they prefer one kid over another it is even steven when it comes to the will. The rest plan to base their largesse on their children's individual needs and their own individual feelings for them.

WIGGLE OUT OF PAYING THE BILLS?

More women (72 percent) than men (52 percent) get stuck with writing the checks, according to American Express. On average the process eats up six hours a month. Men are almost twice as likely as women (59 v. 32 percent) to pay bills without reviewing them.

WHAT'S MORE FUN . . .
MAKING MONEY OR SPENDING IT?

Perhaps surprising, guys enjoy making money more than they do spending it (40 percent to 22 percent). While just 15 percent believe strongly that money can buy happiness, almost universally they believe its absence is a sure ticket to unhappiness. More men say the pleasure of growing money exceeds the pain of losing it. Men think about money almost as much as they think about sex though only 35 percent admit that they enjoy sex more than they enjoy money.

DOES MONEY YOU'VE EARNED MAKE YOU HAPPIER THAN AN INHERITANCE OR WINDFALL?

Fifty-two percent of men find the proceeds from the sweat of their own brow *is* sweeter. But 63 percent also say they get as much enjoyment from their spouse's money as they do from their own.

HOW GENEROUS ARE YOU SHARING IT?

During a typical year two out of three guys give money to a charity, although collectively women are likelier to be considerably more generous. Seventeen percent of men claim that they often give money to beggars whom they come across; 16 percent usually give generously beyond the obligatory dollar when the collection plate is passed, and a third have contributed to at least one political campaign. The biggest "official" beneficiary of their largesse is the Salvation Army.

THINK THE MEEK WILL INHERIT THE EARTH?

Only 39 percent of men are buying, according to marketing research firm Alden & Associates. At the same time, 61 percent of men (considerably more than women) believe that people usually get what they deserve and that life is fair.

HOW GOOD ARE YOU AT HANDLING MONEY?

More men think they're far more fiscally skillful than their financial statements indicate: more than half believe they're better than average at beating the market. Research shows that 88 percent of men exaggerate their returns. Despite a dour economy,

51 percent fully expect to recoup any money they've lost during a downturn. Only 15 percent admit they'd be damn jealous if their neighbor or colleague struck it rich.

WHAT KIND OF INVESTOR ARE YOU?

A Wall Street adage has it that men worry about getting a good return on their money, whereas women worry about getting their money returned. Men tend to be abrupt and impulsive investors. Rather than riding the bunny hill at first, they plunge down the double diamonds, taking risks, acting independently, choosing volatile "boy stocks" (i.e., high-techs, energy, and manufacturing), and exuding confidence because they are bluffing (or kidding themselves), says Paine Webber Vice President Mike Saunders. Meanwhile, women often suffer from paralysis by analysis and lean toward "girl stocks," retailers and consumer products. Men need to see on average 18 multimedia impressions to understand a product's benefits and make a decision; women need only five impressions, says Paul Lucas, formerly marketing vice president at First Advantage Federal Credit Union.

BEEN BITTEN BY THE GAMBLING BUG?

Sixty-eight percent have risked some money somehow at least once in the past year. Some 29 percent would rather take their chances at the craps table than on a new stock offering. For them IPO means "it's probably overpriced." Sixty-two percent bought a lottery ticket at least once and 57 percent have done so in the past year. Men are more seduced by the size of the jackpot than by their odds of winning. Thirty percent have been to a casino in the past year. Here they're more likely to play blackjack than anything else. Just one percent play Keno. The average man sets a $300 risk limit for one visit, but 11 percent, at least once, have lost more than their predetermined quit amount. Only four percent of men are compulsive gamblers.

GOT A BUDGET? HOW ABOUT AN EMERGENCY FUND?

Just 43 percent of men stick to a monthly budget most or all of the time; 43 percent have never established one. Forty-four percent concede that money flows out of their hands almost as quickly as it flows in. Despite the likelihood that they'll need to tap some cash to get through a rough patch, only 40 percent have established an emergency fund.

DO YOU USUALLY BUY THE CHEAPEST SEATS AT A GAME AND THEN TRY TO SCOOT UP TO BETTER ONES?

More than three out of four men—77 percent—would rather shell out more money and be sure they had good seats. Only 23 percent try to upgrade themselves at the stadium or theater.

DOES CROESUS PLAY A PART IN YOUR DAYDREAMS?

Just about half of men (49 percent) daydream of riches. But that is three times as many as those who dream of fame or of being great at their profession.

What Would You Do For Money?

- ➤ 66 percent would live on a deserted island for a year for $1 million.

- 60 percent would take the rap for someone else and serve six months in jail.
- 7 percent would commit murder for $3 million.
- 22 percent would go up against a heavyweight boxer for a $100,000 payout.
- 7 percent would marry for money.
- 64 percent would blab something they promised a best friend to keep secret for $3,000.
- 58 percent would go homeless, sleeping on the street for a week for $2,000.
- 59 percent would shave their heads for $10,000.
- 21 percent would swallow a worm for $300.
- 25 percent would abandon their friends and home and change their race or sex for $10 million.

What Particular Frugalities Do You Practice?

- 56 percent of men always top off the gas tank before returning a rental car.
- 59 percent have stayed over on a Saturday night to take advantage of a discount airfare. Even more have taken multiple stop airplane routes to save on the cost of the ticket.
- 24 percent reuse tea bags.
- 39 percent let the discounts determine when they make their phone calls.
- 10 percent transfer stuff from a private label box into a brand name container to make it look richer.
- 20 percent make ice cubes way before a party so as not to have to buy them.
- 40 percent regularly call hotels to negotiate better rates if they're paying.
- 25 percent have switched credit cards in the last year to pay a lower interest rate or avoid forking over an annual fee.

➤ 34 percent would drive out of their way for cheaper gas.

➤ 14 percent dilute ketchup with water to coax out the remnants.

➤ 64 percent use a bar of soap until it's a mere sliver.

➤ 60 percent get inventive squeezing the contents out of the toothpaste tube.

➤ 54 percent regard themselves as allergic to playing full price: they *always* look for a bargain.

➤ 55 percent would sit in the middle coach seat for a five-hour flight rather than shell out an extra $100 to sit in business class.

7

Between the Sheets

GOT PENIS ENVY?

The average man's erect penis stretches 5.877 inches, about the size of a medium cup of coffee at Starbucks, while stubby ones measure in at 2.4 inches and lengthy ones at 11 inches. A third of men would have their penis enlarged if the procedure didn't hurt or cost anything. More than four out of five guys have measured themselves. Sixteen percent consider themselves "well endowed"; 12 percent suspect they're on the small size.

HOW FRISKY ARE YOU?

The average man has sex 138 times a year, spending 28 minutes a session on it, counting foreplay and the actual act (though with a long-standing partner the session lasts on average 16 minutes). The mean for married men (of all ages) is around six times a month: most would like it twice that often. The main reason for the disparity is no longer headaches: it's fatigue. Sixteen percent of men claim they usually have multiple orgasms.

WHEN DID THE WHOLE THING START?

Most American guys lose their virginity around age 16. For 34 percent the first time was unplanned: things went further than they'd expected (hoped). Seventeen percent married the first partner with whom they had sex.

HOW KINKY?

Almost one in five guys use porn to spice up the sex act. Eight percent have tied up a partner or been tied up themselves. And 36 percent call their organs cutesy names.

ARE YOU PREOCCUPIED WITH SEX?

The average Joe spends 730 hours a year musing about sex—and 22 hours a year having it. Fifty-four percent say they think about sex at least once a day. Half were so desperate that they've had sex with someone for whom they had absolutely no feelings. Seventeen percent own up to having kept a dating partner past her expiration date for sex on a regular basis. Twenty-seven percent have done it with someone out of pity. Yet, 52 percent consider sex overrated: often they'd rather play soccer or go to the gym. Eleven percent can imagine going through life celibate and without regrets.

HOW WELL DO YOU NEED TO
KNOW SOMEONE BEFORE DOING IT?

Men are 10 times likelier than women to consider it more than okay to get down to business on the first date. One in five thinks that's fine while 12 percent each thinks it's better to wait until the second or third date. Five percent believe sex should wait until after marriage.

EVER DONE IT WITH ANOTHER MAN?

By one count, 6.3 percent of men have—twice the percent of women who have had same sex relationships.

HOW MANY NOTCHES ON YOUR BELT?

The average man has 17 lovers in his lifetime. Ninety-two percent have at least 10. Fifty-one percent can't recall the first and last name of each sexual partner. Four percent have had sex with a total stranger.

SO WHAT'S MISSING?

Sixty percent of men would love more variety in their lovemaking—you know what that means—and 30 percent want to hear sweet nothings from their partner.

EVER DONE IT IN A CAR?

Sure, almost everyone has, but one in five claims to have done it while driving. One in five says he's had a sexual experience in the back of a cab.

WHERE ELSE? WHEN?

Thirteen percent claim membership in the mile-high club and two out of three have done it in a hot tub. Despite the sand, 62 percent have done it on the beach and 83 percent in some other public place. The most popular time for sex is late Saturday evening. Monday afternoon is the least popular time.

TEND TO NOD OFF RIGHT AFTER?

Men plead the fifth here, but one in three women complain about this inevitability. Most accept it somewhat graciously, however.

ARE YOU A HOT KISSER?

Half of men consider kissing more intimate than the act itself. Thirty-eight percent prefer to do it with their eyes open, and two out of three slant to the right when locking lips. More than one in three (37 percent) have a decided preference for no lipstick, but if the woman must wear it, make it strawberry-flavored.

DO YOU TAKE MATTERS INTO YOUR OWN HANDS?

Nearly 85 percent of men in a relationship secretly pleasure themselves. Although masturbation causes no harm, four out of five men remember being told the terrors that would befall them if they "played with it"—that they'd become cross-eyed, blind, deaf, or crazy, that hair would grow on their hands, or that "it" would fall off.

PAID FOR IT?

Nineteen percent of men reveal they have called a sex hotline. Fewer than one in three has ever hired a prostitute. Forty percent would consider having sex for money and half could imagine themselves getting paid to pose nude in a magazine.

SOLD BY IT?

That depends on your age. Research shows that young adults are more likely to buy some items like clothing if ads blare raunchiness, but sex doesn't work to sell furniture or appliances. Overall, experts say 36 percent of men—especially those not in committed relationships—pay more attention to sexy ads than to mainstream advertising. Yet 45 percent of men say they're offended by ads that use sex to sell.

BEEN A CHEATER OR CHEAT-EE?

By one count, 34 percent of men have been cuckolded. Statistics suggest that men were twice as likely as women to cheat if they knew they'd get away with it. But 43 percent of cheaters feel tormented after the fact (though not always enough to confess or end the affair). Two-thirds of men say their mainstay is a better bedmate than their flings. More than six out of 10 men acknowledge that they have had the occasional doubt about the parentage of their child.

HOW ABOUT A RAKE?

Seems they abound. Sixty percent of men have had at least one one-night stand. Forty-two percent have had sex with two different women on the same day. Thirty percent have had sex with a friend of their girlfriend. Eighteen percent have faked it because they were secretly no longer into their partner but not ready to deal with the drama of breaking up.

AND LIAR?

Nearly 70 percent have made up stories about past sexual romps. Fourteen percent admit to faking an orgasm. Half have lied to get a date, most likely about their willingness to commit, their interest in more than just sex, and their income.

GOT ANY, AHEM, PERFORMANCE PROBLEM?

Collectively, guys stand a one in three chance of falling down on the job, but the likelihood of that happening increases by 300 percent after age 50.

GOT ANY PROBLEMS FROM YOUR PERFORMANCE?

One in every six men has had a sexually transmitted disease and one in five is infected with the virus that causes genital herpes, though it's likely that he doesn't know it. Thirty-nine percent had unprotected sex with a new partner in a recent year.

WORRY ABOUT HOW GOOD YOU ARE IN BED?

Two in every five guys worry about being able to perform. Nine percent have been sorely wounded when a partner told them that they weren't pleasuring her adequately. While 44 percent of men say their partner saw stars during sex, only 29 percent of those women actually did.

According to IKEA:

- 21 percent of guys have had sex in their kitchen, with those having recently renovated their kitchen more likely to score where they cook.
- Oddly, guys who wear aprons are twice as likely to have sex there as those who go apron-less.
- Men with messy sock drawers have sex three times more a month than those whose sock bins are organized. (Then again, couples without closet organizers argue three times less each month than those who have them.)

THINK GREAT SEX CAN TRIGGER LOVE?

Women disagree but 46 percent of men say it can—and has—because one's behavior during sex reveals a lot about one's character. At the same time, men agree that bad sex can trigger a breakup as it's often indicative of selfishness. Forty-six percent of men say they have developed committed relationships from one-night stands.

WHAT BODY TYPE TICKLES YOUR FANCY?

Men may snicker about voluptuous breasts but 81 percent of them prefer that their own partner have medium-sized ones. Only 14 percent find bigger better. More men are attracted to the shape of a woman's legs than by her cup size. Fifty-seven percent are more apt to wind up with someone who is very much like them rather than someone who is very different. The ideal woman is of average height, with blue eyes, full lips, and wavy, shoulder-length brown hair.

TURNED ON BY THE CHASE?

Sixty percent of men find the challenge stimulating, but 40 percent don't think jumping through hoops is worth their time or effort. And they consider the person who makes them do it unworthy.

TURNED OFF BY THE FIGHTING?

Surely not the 22 percent of men who claim their fights usually resolve in the sack. Most men, however, talk out the issue rather than lust it away. Then again, almost a half of guys in long-term relationships go tight-lipped for a while.

WHAT CONSTITUTES INFIDELITY?

Men have a fairly loose standard. Eighty-eight percent consider only their partner having intercourse with another man to qualify. Seventy-eight percent consider fondling another indicative of infidelity, while 51 percent consider kissing someone else an act of infidelity. Just shy of half rank phone sex in this class and 42 percent would similarly classify cybersex. Just one in three men would draw the line at holding hands with another and 17 percent would include lustfully thinking about another. Sixteen percent regard flirting as cheating and six percent—sensitive sorts—view looking at another in this category.

CARRY A CONDOM?

Seventy-four percent of men wish they should be so lucky. Nine percent tote one around but are embarrassed to say how long it's been in their wallet. Seventeen percent regularly replace the one they carry around. Forty-one percent of those who carry a condom tuck it in their wallet.

Bedtime

The average American man spends around the same amount of time sleeping as he does working. It takes him on average seven minutes to fall asleep.

- Just about the same number sleep on their left side as on their right, considerably more than who sleep on their stomach or on their back.
- 43 percent use two pillows; 37 percent use one.
- Two out of three in happy relationships often start off spooning, then gradually separate.
- Two out of three prefer a firm to a soft mattress.
- 41 percent prefer a standard double to any other size.
- 6 percent prefer twin beds.
- 60 percent of men use a cover even in hot weather.
- 16 percent leave a night-light on when they're in a strange bed.
- 47 percent consider themselves larks (v. 42 percent owls).
- 48 percent of dog owners welcome Rover into the sheets.
- 26 percent lock their bedroom door when they go to sleep.
- 26 percent go to bed between 11:00 P.M. and midnight; just 15 percent hit the sack before 10:00 P.M.
- Most wake up briefly at least five times during the night but are probably unaware of these periods of wakefulness.
- Three out of four have a favorite side of the bed that they stick to even in hotels.
- 90 percent need the jolt of an alarm clock to wake up: of those, half have it set to music or a buzzer, just five percent to news.

8

With Family and Friends: Kids, Partners, Parents, and Friends

Pas De Deux

SHARE YOUR DREAMS WITH HER?

Nearly one in five guys (19 percent) keeps a secret dream or goal that he does not talk about with his lady. But 47 percent of those who have gone from friend to lover have few secrets. On the other hand, three out of 10 husbands and wives are in the dark about how much each other earns. Thirty-six percent keep separate bank accounts. More than 60 percent hoard a private cash cache to safeguard against the possibility of a breakup.

WOULD YOU RELOCATE IF YOUR PARTNER WERE TRANSFERRED?

Three out of four women (73 percent) say they would pack up and go, even if not happily. But only 36 percent of men admit that they would make that sacrifice.

HOW'D YOU FEEL ABOUT
A WIFE WHO OUTEARNS YOU?

Way to go, say 69 percent of men. But only 38 percent would feel comfortable being a stay-at-home dad.

WOULD YOU, OR DID YOU, TAKE PATERNITY LEAVE?

A recent U.S. Department of Labor survey found a third of new fathers took some leave after they brought home a newborn. More relied on "underground leave," time scraped together with vacation or sick days. The average new dad takes off less than a week. Three of every four men worry that staying away any longer could crimp their income or hurt their career.

HOW FORGETFUL ARE YOU?

Fully 22 percent of guys have forgotten their wedding anniversaries, double the percent of guilty women. Western men suffer the greatest memory lapses and longtime marrieds are far more likely than newlyweds to lose sight of the occasion. Those earning the least were the least likely to forget.

ASK YOUR PARTNER'S PERMISSION
TO GO OUT WITH THE BOYS?

Nah, say 62 percent of guys who figure they're not in relationships to date their mothers. But 37 percent feel that when a house and kids are involved and someone else has to pull his weight when he's not doing it, it's best to register for a leave and that it has nothing to do with men being dominated. Similarly most men consult with their partner before buying something big.

THEM OR HER?

Nearly three in four men (73 percent) would prefer to spend a romantic evening in, with his sweetie, than a raucous one out with the boys. Amazingly, married men are 14 percent more likely than unmarried men to prefer an intimate night home. Four out of ten men often use the magic words "love you" to end a phone call.

WHAT DO YOU AND YOUR LADY FIGHT ABOUT?

The number one cause of couple conflict is money. Twenty-nine percent of married men argue more about their spouse's spending habits than anything else. The second most hotly contested issue: whether to watch *Fear Factor* or *The Apprentice*.

BATTLE IN THE BATHROOM?

Sharing a water closet can wither a relationship. Men find it especially rattling when their beloved consistently fails to replace the toilet paper when the roll runs out on their clock. While women sputter with indignation over men not wiping down the tub after they use it, men are also significantly miffed about all the stuff cluttering up the shower and by the hair left in the drain or on the soap, and wet towels on the floor.

WHAT DO YOU DO IN A LOVER'S SPAT?

Almost half of all guys slam doors and more than one in three rant and rave. Seventeen percent often throw or break things, but none own up to hitting their sparring partner. Twenty-one percent serve up the silent treatment for a day or more. Twelve percent have withheld sex as punishment after an argument, according to adult products company Adam & Eve. Twenty-two percent of women pull that number.

WHO WINS THE WAR?

That depends on what the battle is about. When it comes to disciplining the kids, running the house, or planning time together, the lady usually gets the last word. Husbands usually prevail when it comes to which friends to socialize with and which TV programs to watch. Financial fights often end in a draw. Forty-three percent of men say they hardly ever spar with their partner, but one in five feels that he is taken for granted.

DO YOU WATCH FOOTBALL WITH YOUR OTHER HALF?

The Janet Jackson wardrobe malfunction notwithstanding, the NFL is good family fare to be enjoyed with the woman, say 52 percent of M-I-R (men in relationships). But 48 percent retreat to their private den, garage, or local sports bar and surface in February.

DO YOU AND YOUR PARTNER USUALLY VOTE THE SAME WAY?

Two out of three couples almost always cast the same vote in national and local elections.

WHEN YOU HOLD HANDS, WHO HAS THE UPPER HAND?

That depends largely on who's taller. Temple University psychologist Mark Chapell found that more than nine out of 10 times, when the man was estimated to be at least an inch taller than the woman, the guy's hand was in front and uppermost. When the couples are roughly the same height, the man's hand was higher than his sweetheart's about 86 percent of the time. But when the guy was more than an inch shorter than his sweetheart, the man's hand was uppermost half the time and the woman's was on top the other half.

WHAT MAKES MARRIEDS INCOMPATIBLE?

Three out of four men feel if they and their intended can't agree on whether to have kids they should call it quits. More than half feel they've got to be able to chime in bed before doing it in a church. Forty-four percent say different spending styles lead to big trouble and 18 percent feel similar racial, ethnic, religious backgrounds and political views are vital to make a marriage work.

DID YOU PROPOSE ON BENDED KNEE?

Fewer than one in every five guys has knelt to present a ring. Even less—four percent—have sought parental—approval. National Jeweler found men are likeliest to pop the question in December and June with February as a close third, and buy an engagement ring in December. Once the ring has been given, most couples stay engaged for a half year or less before tying the knot. Low-wage earners are likeliest to have the longest engagements. In two out of three purchases, the groom and bride-to-be shop for the ring together. Solitaires are the most popular style.

WOULD YOU CHOOSE THE SAME LASS IF YOU COULD REDO IT?

Four out of five men profess they would marry the same woman if they had it to do all over again. Only half of the women would walk down that same aisle with her husband.

WOULD YOU LET YOUR WEDDING BE "SPONSORED"?

Practicality reigns. While women are less likely to go for having a commercial organization pay their way in exchange for publicity, almost half (49 percent) of all men feel it's a good swap. One in four husbands has taken out a loan to pay for the wedding and honeymoon.

GOT A PRENUP?

While some guys think you can't really be in love if you need a prenuptial agreement, 53 percent say that in this day and age it's necessary to protect against gold diggers and that any potential mate who won't sign one is after their wallet. Still, 47 percent feel that the concept of a prenup and a lasting marriage are mutually exclusive.

HOW OFTEN HAVE YOU FALLEN IN LOVE?

In a lifetime, the average man falls in love six times, starting with puppy love around age 13 and a "serious" relationship at 17. Forty-four percent claim to have fallen in love at first sight.

ARE YOU LIKELIER TO FOLLOW
YOUR HEAD OR YOUR HEART?

Your head may derail a partnership, but emotion still ultimately instigates it. Overwhelmingly, men say that for them pairing up is prompted by their hearts. Yet at the same time, 63 percent say that it's possible (and smart) to direct and govern whom you fall for.

IF THE DUO NEEDS DARNING,
IS IT WORTH THE TROUBLE?

When there's considerable emotional capital on the table, 89 percent of men think it justifies a greater investment. Only 11 percent feel that if a relationship has soured, it's better to cut the cord and move on to something sweeter.

WHO WOULD YOU DATE? AVOID?

Seventy-eight percent of guys would have no problem dating someone of a different race and 89 percent would happily go out with a woman up to five years his senior. Only 46 percent would spend time with someone they find unattractive. An equal number would and would not date someone with young children. Thirty-eight percent would shy away from someone with a sexually transmitted disease (assuming they knew) and half would shirk a potential partner with a low sex drive. Ninety percent would avoid a smoker, and 84 percent, a relationship with a friend's estranged spouse.

WHERE WOULD YOU GO ON A FIRST DATE?

Out to dinner at a restaurant is the overwhelming favorite. But 12 percent of guys would test the waters at the movies and 11 percent would make their debut as a duo at a play. Seven percent would hope to meet up at a bar and three percent would try to arrange a walk, picnic, or something else outdoors.

WOULD YOU TRUST YOUR MOM TO SET YOU UP?

Fifty-seven percent of guys looking to connect would steer clear of dating agencies, but even more—74 percent—would give mom wide berth when it comes to prospecting for them. Half of guys looking for love have placed a personal ad or responded to seductive ads from others. Nearly three out of four mention their weight in the ad; only 43 percent of women do. It takes a woman on average an hour to determine if she's in for round two; the typical guy decides in 15 minutes. Sixty-two percent of guys wait just a day or two to call for a follow-up date. Half of single guys (49 percent) consider themselves commitment-phobic.

AND IF SHE'S GAINED SOME HEFT?

While three out of four women say they would have a relationship with a heavyset man, 35 percent of men would avoid one with a Rubenesque woman. Six percent of men have ended a relationship solely because the partner in it has packed on the pounds. And six percent have been dumped because of their girth.

BREAKUP STRATEGY?

More than half of men (53 percent) prefer the harsh truth rather than being fed a gentle white lie. A third of men have begged their executioner to take them back.

WHEN ENDING A RELATIONSHIP, DO YOU USUALLY FADE AWAY?

Many more men confront their partner with news that they're dumping her (48 percent) than disappear into the woodwork (34 percent). More than half of those who face the music hope to salvage a friendship. Fourteen percent try to cleverly engineer it so she ends the relationship while four percent plot a fight that scuttles things.

STRATEGY FOR DEALING WITH AN EX?

More than 60 percent have crafted an opportunity to make their ex jealous; 21 percent have exacted some sort of revenge for being dumped. Forty-two percent would return to an ex for sex; 24 percent have done so already. Sixty-two percent of guys muse about getting back together with a former lover. Indeed, 16 percent say they think of someone they once loved almost every day. (Just 24 percent cut bait and move on.) Only 35 percent keep in touch with their ex. Forty-three percent are cool with their current partner maintaining a (platonic) relationship with her ex. Seventy-one percent would be miffed if a good friend took up with his former girl.

BEEN BROKENHEARTED?

Ninety-five percent of men have experienced unrequited love before age 25. Men's average "hang time" between serious romances is 15 months while their average "wait" for sex is just over four months. Men are much more likely than women to try to mend a broken heart by dating someone new or getting drunk, while women find cleaning, shopping, and writing in a journal to be therapeutic.

HOW DO YOU EVALUATE ONLINE BAIT?

First thing 56 percent of guys do is check out the photo. Then to determine whether to contact a potential mate they look at where their prospective honey lives, her age, and how well she writes and spells. Three percent also pay attention to the "applicant's" weight and two percent to her profession. One in five men has had a first date shocker—although 73 percent say they've been lied to about body type. Then again, 41 percent of men admit they've stretched the truth in their own online profile, most likely about their body type or desire for children.

LOOKING FOR A MIRROR REFLECTION—OR SOMEONE WAY DIFFERENT?

You know why dogs look like their master? Well, 57 percent of men are more likely to be attracted to a partner who is much like them than someone exotic. Seven out of 10 men want a woman who is sexually open-minded but even more want a partner who cooks just like their mother, according to the Ipsos Institute. Fifty-one percent like a woman slow to boil, temper-wise, and 48 percent would rather never hear "What are you thinking?"

TREAT HER WELL?

For a majority of men, that would be going against the grain. Seventy-nine percent subscribe to the "treat them mean, keep them keen" motto.

MARRIAGE PRONE OR ADVERSE?

Most single young men want to marry, but 23 percent are hard-core commitment-phobic marriage avoiders, according to the National Marriage Project at Rutgers University. Men scared of marriage were far more likely than the rest to have been raised by a divorced parent in a non-churchgoing family. Men say their biggest fear is that their partner will turn into her mother—or, worse, into his mother. Almost one in four focuses on the fact that he'll never be able to have sex with another woman while 19 percent are daunted by Lamaze class and what comes after that. Just four percent shy from marriage for fear that they'll screw it up.

LIKE TO FLIRT?

Eighty-one percent of men flirt with their partner and 45 percent enjoy flirting with others as well—using eye contact to make a connection. While more than two out of every three men swear they never ogle others in front of their partner, 62 percent of women claim they've caught their guys in the act.

DO YOU CARE IF YOUR LADY FRIEND
SLEEPS WITH TEDDY BEARS?

Half of guys are rattled seeing fuzzy pink elephants staring at them. It reminds them that the sexy babe next to them was— and still is—someone's little girl. But almost as many find teddy bears and Beanie Babies sprawled on the bed cute and indicative that the lady likes to cuddle.

WHAT GETS YOU ALL LOVEY-DOVEY?

Men find music from a piano more romantic than any other in-strument, followed by the saxophone and the human voice. But they're almost equally divided over whether being serenaded by a violinist in a restaurant is romantic or annoying. Only 13 per-cent would enjoy being unexpectedly "kidnapped" for a week-end away at a B and B; 87 percent would be peeved.

HOW DO YOU SET THE MOOD?

When feeling amorous at home, men say their favorite mood setters are, in order, cooking their partner's favorite meal, mut-tering sweet nothings, lighting candles, and playing soft music.

DINE WITH YOUR FAMILY
AT LEAST A FEW TIMES A WEEK?

Despite all the talk about fractured lives, 79 percent of families eat together at least two nights a week. Half claim to eat dinner at home with their family almost every night.

ARE YOU A DAD?

Sixty percent of males over the age of 15 are dads, according to the Census Bureau. On average, each claims paternal rights to 1.6 children. Eighty-six percent of male high school seniors say they want to have kids someday. Yet one in every 25 men suffers from infertility and another 500,000 elect to have a vasectomy every year, according to Mediamark Research, Inc.

WOULD YOU OKAY YOUR TEEN DAUGHTER GETTING HER TONGUE PIERCED?

Girlfriend, maybe. Daughter, are you nuts? Eighty-five percent of guys figure pierced tongues are good for one thing—and it's not improving diction. But only 54 percent would be disturbed if their grown child showed up with a tattoo.

DO YOU GIVE YOUR PET HOLIDAY PRESENTS?

Seventy-nine percent of pet owners give their animal companions a holiday treat and 43 percent often give them a birthday gift. Almost half (44 percent) buy souvenirs on vacation to bring home to their pet.

HOW ARE YOU WITH MUM AND DAD?

Sure, one in 10 guys considers Mom the devil incarnate but more than three times that number—34 percent—count her as their soul mate. The majority—56 percent—talk to her once a week, out of politeness or habit. Three out of five guys whose dads are still living profess to have a great relationship with them. Another 24 percent characterize the attachment as a good one while eight percent feel neutral about Pop. Twenty-six percent talk with their dad daily. One in 10 men considers his parents his best friends. More than half of young men (18 to 24) and 44 percent of 35- to 44-year-olds still go to their mum with health worries.

HOW OFTEN DO YOU SEE OTHER RELATIVES?

Counting the times you visit them or host them at your place, the average guy visits with relatives once every few weeks. One in four connects at least once a week and another 27 percent see them once or twice a month. Thirteen percent have not visited any relatives in the past year. Still, 92 percent of men claim they feel good about their relations with their family.

WHAT'S THE IDEAL NUMBER OF KIDS IN A FAMILY?

Two is still the magic number with half of men saying that's the right size. Twenty-six percent prefer three kids and nine percent even more. Just three percent of men would like only one child.

WHO'S THE BAD COP WITH THE KIDS?

"Just wait until your father gets home," seems to be a threat from yesteryear, on par with "Don't make me stop this car." Fathers are more likely to be softies than mothers. Forty-two percent of dads feel that they discipline their kids less often or less severely than their mother does. Fewer than one in three considers himself the sterner parent.

WHAT'S THE FIRST THING YOU DO
WHEN YOU COME HOME?

Four times as many men as women hug their spouse first thing when they walk in the door after work. Most immediately kick off their shoes when they come home. Twenty percent hasten to change their clothes while 10 percent listen to their phone messages and another 10 percent open the mail. The kids, spouse, and pet get equal priority: eight percent each hug their offspring, kiss their mate, and attend to their pet. Two percent head straight to the stove. Fewer than one percent turn on the computer, TV, or radio.

WHO DO YOU CALL MOST OFTEN?

It isn't the old lady. Guys are much more likely to reach for the phone to talk about something job-related, so work colleagues including their secretary (should they be so lucky) and boss get rung up most often. Their mate comes in third, ahead of friends, parents, and kids.

WHO ARE YOU MOST LIKELY TO
SLAM THE PHONE ON?

The ex-flame that has extinguished is likeliest to get you to hang up . . . but close behind is your current hottie. More than one in three guys have at some point in their relationships hung up on their mother-in-law.

HOW DO YOU FEEL ABOUT YOUR MOTHER-IN-LAW?

Despite the stereotype of meddling mothers-in-law for whom no prince is good enough for their daughter, almost nine in 10 guys say they get along fine with their partner's female parent.

BEEN ACTIVE IN THE COMMUNITY?

One in five men has been involved in the past 12 months in neighborhood groups such as a block association, a homeowner or tenant association, or a crime watch group.

WHEN YOU EAT OUT WITH FRIENDS DO YOU SPLIT THE CHECK?

Forty-eight percent divvy the tab equally. For 21 percent, whoever is treating, treats, while 27 percent chip in proportionally to what they've ordered.

WITH GOOD FRIENDS DO YOU KEEP SCORE OF WHO PAYS FOR WHAT?

Forget about a mental scorecard. Four percent actually write it down. Forty-four percent figure it evens out in the end, while one in five doesn't care who spends more—that the friendship is more important than who pays for what.

HOW ABOUT ON A DATE?

Three out of four people think the guy should pay for dinner if he has invited a woman out on a date. Eight percent think the couple should split the check and two percent consider it only fair that the person who earns the most money should pay.

HOW OFTEN DO YOU LUNCH WITH COWORKERS?

Thirteen percent of workers say they do so every day while three percent wouldn't be caught dead sharing the table. Thirty-six percent eat together once or twice a week and 31 percent sit down a few times a month.

YOU BIG WITH GREETING CARDS?

If it weren't for women the industry would have tanked. Still, 82 percent of men have sent at least one card in the past year and 24 percent have mailed more than a dozen (v. 45 percent of women). Twenty-seven percent of men keep the cards they receive (v. 49 percent of women).

LIVE ON E-MAIL?

Two out of three men say most of their relationships are conducted online. Fifty-one percent of those who use e-mail at work check it at least once an hour; indeed, 32 percent check it continuously. Only five percent log on less than once a day. At home, most guys check their e-mail a couple of times a day. Men, even more than women, claim to hate spam (45 percent).

WHAT PRICE FRIENDSHIP?

Three out of four men say they'd lend their best friend $1,000 if asked (assuming they had the dough), but only 59 percent have been hit up for any size loan. Seventy-one percent say they'd put their life on the line for a best bud—with two out of three avowing they'd donate bone marrow or an organ to a desperate, albeit very close friend. While 79 percent would let a friend in a jam move in for a while, just 56 percent would welcome them as a long-term roommate.

HOW MANY FRIENDS IN YOUR COLUMN?

Two-thirds say they have enough friends to brighten their lives. The average Joe has at least 14 close friends, including a best bud, but sees only four regularly. Fifty-three percent of men consider their wife or S.O. to be their best friend. For 88 percent of men, their best friend is another man. Just 18 percent have a platonic friendship with a member of the opposite sex. Just 28 percent have a best friend who is more than five years younger or older than they are.

HOW LONG HAVE YOU KNOWN YOUR BEST FRIEND?

The typical guy has known his best friend for 14 years. Two out of three have been friends for at least a decade. Twelve percent have ended a long-term friendship because of something unacceptable their erstwhile buddy did.

ARE YOU A GOOD FRIEND?

Most guys think they are lending an ear and hand when needed. They believe they've earned the friendship by being truthful and trustworthy, kind and fun. But 46 percent admit that despite their best intentions and promises, they've betrayed a friend's confidence.

HOW ABOUT A GOOD NEIGHBOR?

Three out of four men (77 percent) feel connected to their communities. The same percent consider their next-door neighbors to be friends and have helped or been helped by a neighbor in an emergency. Yet one in three guys has had a fight with a neighbor, most likely because of the way they treated their (or his) property or the racket they've made.

9

Behind the Wheel

The typical American man spends 2.5 hours a day in a car, drives 16,408 miles a year, and will spend two weeks of his life waiting for traffic lights to change and $7,215 a year to keep those wheels turning. Fourteen percent currently own or lease a car with side air bags.

DO YOU STOP AT THE YELLOW OR SPEED UP AT THEM?

Two out of three guys see a yellow light and floor it. Northeasterners are, surprisingly, more likely to stop at a yellow traffic light than Midwesterners.

BREAK INTO A SWEAT WHEN PARKING IN A TIGHT SPOT?

Assuming there's a long line of cars waiting behind you, one out of every ten men confesses he suffers from damp armpits in this situation.

TALK TO YOUR CAR?

Some 55 percent of men and 45 percent of women talk to their car. Two out of three call their wheels by a pet name and 12 percent have even "christened" the car for good luck. Fifty-three percent carry around a photo of their car or keep it on their desk at work. Goodyear found that 32 percent of men swear at their car and 22 percent have implored it to keep going when they feared it was running out of gas. Twenty-six percent thank their car for a job well done.

FILL IT WITH PREMIUM?

Fewer than one in 10 cars on the road actually require high octane gas but one in five guys pumps it into their baby anyway, shelling out at least 17 cents more per gallon than necessary. Forty-five percent fill up with regular, and 17 percent consistently opt for the cheapest.

CHOOSE A FUEL-INJECTED SPORTS CAR OR AN AIRBRUSHED CELEBRITY?

The Lamborghini or Ferrari easily trump Britney Spears or Pamela Anderson as a companion for the weekend. Eighty-six percent of men chose the Ferrari over Anderson, and 74 percent would rather cuddle with a Lamborghini than with Spears.

WHAT DO YOU DO WHEN YOU'RE LOST OR CONFUSED WHEN DRIVING?

Big surprise: more women (38 percent) than men (21 percent) just kept on driving, hoping for divine intervention of a marker they recognize. Of those who do seek help, 59 percent of men and 46 percent of women usually stop at a gas station for directions. Thirty-five percent pull out a map to figure out where they're going.

WHAT IS YOUR FAVORITE CAR COLOR?

Blue is the favorite color among men overall but on their wheels it's silver. Close behind is black and then by a considerable distance white, and then gray. A third of men have no set preference other than that their car be a fun shade.

WHAT DO YOU DO WHEN ANOTHER DRIVER CUTS YOU OFF?

Just over half of male drivers—54 percent—don't do a thing. Fifteen percent of the hot-tempered yell an obscenity, seven percent give the offending driver the finger, and three percent of madmen tailgate them in retaliation.

DO YOU ALWAYS OBEY THE SPEED LIMITS?

Posted limits are way too restraining, say two out of three men. Forty-two percent have sailed along at over 90 miles an hour. According to the U.S. Federal Highway Administration, the heaviest concentration of lead-foots are in Arizona, Rhode Island, Vermont, and New Hampshire, and the pokiest, in West Virginia, Virginia, Hawaii, and Kentucky.

EVER RUN OUT OF GAS?

Forty-six percent of drivers overall have stalled on empty, but 59 percent of men have at least once in their life. While for most men a quarter tank signals it's time to pull in, 19 percent wait until they're driving on fumes—when their car's fuel light comes on.

FLASH LIGHTS TO WARN ONCOMING TRAFFIC OF A POLICE TRAP?

Almost four out of every ten people routinely do this courtesy, but men are far likelier than women to warn oncoming traffic to slow down.

CAN YOU CHANGE A FLAT?

Almost universally men say they can (97 percent) but at least one in five has never actually had to change a tire. One in two has dealt with a flat in the past year.

CONSIDER YOURSELF A "WHITE-KNUCKLE" PASSENGER?

While 86 percent of men think that they themselves are excellent drivers (despite the fact that just 35 percent of them drive with both hands on the wheel), 83 percent worry that few other drivers are paying enough attention to the road, or are too angry, tipsy, tired, old, young, or otherwise out of it to get the job done right.

DO YOU DRINK COFFEE WHILE
TOOLING DOWN THE HIGHWAY?

There's a reason car manufacturers have installed cup holders. Eighty-three percent of motorists drink coffee, juice, or soda while driving. (Only 10 percent never touch a morsel while behind the wheel.) Yet 13 percent of rocket scientists hold the soda in their lap or balance it on the dashboard rather than use the cup holders.

LATE AT NIGHT DO YOU
USUALLY STOP AT STOP SIGNS?

Bedeviled by the idea of the cop waiting behind the hedge, 86 percent of guys stop. Red lights are another story. Motor associations say the average person will jump 181 red lights in his or her lifetime.

ALWAYS WEAR YOUR SEAT BELT?

You know you should, of course, but one in five guys still resists. Forty-six percent of pickup truck occupants don't buckle up.

EVER FOLLOW AN AMBULANCE
TO GET THROUGH TRAFFIC FASTER?

While just about one in six drivers hitches the traffic-cutting ride, men are more than twice as likely as women to ride an ambulance's coattails.

THINK OF YOUR CAR AS A ROLLING SINGLES CLUB?

Sixty-two percent of guys have at one point in their life used their car as a flirtation station. Thirty-one percent have cast sidelong glances from the driver's seat or revved their engines to result in a date. Twenty-six percent have followed another driver in hopes of getting to know her.

WHAT HAPPENS WHEN YOU AND
JOE SCHMO REACH A PRIME PARKING SPOT AT
A CROWDED MALL AT THE SAME TIME?

Almost two-thirds of guys will fight for it. Only about a quarter of men and a third of all women will graciously relinquish it. Perhaps because in the Northeast where free parking places are at a premium, male drivers are more aggressive than elsewhere: 79 percent would rather fight compared to 40 percent of Midwesterners.

TAILGATE THINKING YOU CAN
MAKE THE CAR AHEAD GO FASTER?

Forty-four percent of men (and 30 percent of women) admit they occasionally tailgate hoping to speed up the car ahead of them.

EVER TRIED TO WHEEDLE OUT OF A TICKET?

Surprisingly, men are more likely to try this than women. More than four out of every ten men confess to lying, wheedling, cajoling, or resorting to some other subterfuge to avoid getting a ticket.

CAN YOU DRIVE A STICK SHIFT?

Seventy-one percent of guys boast they can.

EVER DRIVE AFTER YOU DRINK?

Alarmingly, one driver in four admits to having driven with a buzz. Fifty-three percent have served as a designated driver and/or been driven home by one.

DO YOU DO IT IN THE ROAD?

Sing, that is. More men sing in the car (78 percent) than belt it out in the bathroom (48 percent). Three out of four who play the car radio while driving also sing along with it. (And yes, more than half of men have had sex in the car.)

HOW OFTEN DO YOU WASH YOUR CAR?

Five percent of men who own cars never give them a rinse, but 22 percent do so religiously—once a week. More people wash their cars in their own driveways than use a commercial car wash.

EVER USED THE "WE MUST BE LOST" LINE?

Assuming it's make-out time, that's the most popular lame line followed by "Must be engine trouble" or "Uh, out of gas"; or "Must be a flat tire" and "It looks like the battery is dead."

WHERE ON THE FAMILY LINEUP
DOES BESSIE COME?

More than one in four guys—27 percent—love their cars more than they do their mother-in-law. One in 10 guys considers his car more important than his spouse and six percent rate them as more important to them than their kids.

DO YOU MIND WHEN
SOMEONE ELSE TAKES IT FOR A SPIN?

Mind would be an understatement: 71 percent of men are so protective of their car that they'd *really* rather no one else drives it. Half even assiduously avoid valet parking so as not to share the driver's seat.

DO YOU USUALLY BUY IT HOLIDAY GIFTS?

For most men that would be going too far, but 12 percent have treated their wheels to a Valentine's Day gift. And if they could afford only one item, they are almost three times more likely to buy a new car stereo (42 percent) and over two times more likely to have their car detailed (34 percent) than they are to buy expensive perfume or cologne for their sweetie pie (15 percent). Truck owners, it seems, are the most devoted: 22 percent celebrate Valentine's Day with their vehicle compared to nine percent of those who own luxury or full-size vehicles and six percent of SUV owners.

JUDGE SOMEONE BY HIS CAR?

Of course it's superficial, but 30 percent of men judge dates by the type of car they drive. One in four has even borrowed someone else's car to impress someone. And 86 percent have washed or prepped their vehicle in some way before picking up a date. Thirty-seven percent of women would like to see a sports car pull up in their driveway while 27 percent hope he turns up in a luxury car, and 17 percent, in a limo.

EVER NOD OFF BEHIND THE WHEEL?

More than one in 10 drivers acknowledges having fallen asleep at the wheel, and twice as many say they have momentarily dozed while driving, according to Farmers Insurance. Almost three times as many men (16 percent) as women have experienced this. Forty-one percent have kept driving when feeling drowsy. Most commonly, however, they pull over for a nap or switch drivers, open the windows or blast the air-conditioning, turn up the radio or CD, and stop for a bite or a cup of joe.

USUALLY LOCK THE CAR?

Twenty percent of drivers more often than not leave their cars unlocked; six percent leave them with the keys in them. The average driver gets locked out of his car nine times in a lifetime.

DETOUR OR STAY PUT?

When faced with a bottleneck, two out of three drivers will take a detour or change lanes just to keep the car moving. More than

40 percent usually take an alternative route when they're apprised of trouble ahead.

WHAT ELSE DO YOU DO IN GRIDLOCK?

Drivers have become so accustomed to stop-and-go traffic that they're good at using delay time productively. Half of men stuck in gridlock have turned it into a romantic encounter. Forty-one percent have groomed themselves—styling their hair or flossing their teeth. Some inventive ones have even cooked on the heated car engine.

WHICH COULD YOU GIVE UP: CARS, PHONES, TV, OR COMPUTERS?

More than three out of four men claim they couldn't make do without their wheels. That beat out a phone on the fritz and a malfunctioning computer. Eighty-four percent of men say they LOVE their car, especially truck owners, followed by SUV owners, luxury, or full-size vehicle owners, and minivan or station wagon owners.

CHECK THE CAR'S BATTERY?

Three out of five men (60 percent) have checked their car's battery within the past year (v. 35 percent of women). Eighty-five percent have checked the engine oil level compared to 62 percent of women.

HOW ABOUT THE TIRE PRESSURE?

According to the Rubber Manufacturers Association just four percent of men regularly check their tire pressure. Most think they know where to look, but fewer than half actually do. Twenty-seven percent incorrectly believe the sidewall of the tire carries the correct information. It indicates the maximum pressure for the tire, not the optimum pressure. Fewer than one in three know the recommended mileage interval for rotating tires and only 22 percent chose one-sixteenth of an inch as the tread depth at which a tire should be replaced. Women are somewhat likelier than men to worry about tires. Seventy-three percent of drivers keep a tire pressure gauge in their car, but 60 percent have never checked the pressure in their spare.

AND THE WINDSHIELD WIPER FLUID?

Experts suggest that just as you change your smoke detector's battery with daylight saving time, you should check the levels of your car's windshield washer fluid. But fewer than one in five men do this routinely. Most either stock up when there's a sale, or buy it on the road when streaks make vision iffy.

FOLLOW SUGGESTED MAINTENANCE SCHEDULES?

Three out of four men do, although 17 percent acknowledge that they have put off maintaining their vehicle for lack of time, money, or energy. If the engine light comes on, half hasten to get their car serviced the next day. Another 39 percent, more casual customers, wait up to a week to do so to phone for an appointment.

EVER JUST GO FOR A JOYRIDE?

Men are twice as likely as women to take their car for a destination-less spin.

THINK YOUR CAR HAS A PERSONALITY?

Almost three out of four car owners (72 percent) of both genders say their car reflects their personality. Men are more likely than women to classify their car as sexy and aggressive, while more women regard their car as smart and friendly. Surprisingly two out of three truck owners consider their vehicle to be female compared to 37 percent of SUV owners.

BEEN PULLED OVER RECENTLY?

One in every 10 of the 186.3 million licensed drivers in America, some 19.3 million of them, have been stopped by police in a recent year and 69 percent of those unfortunates received a ticket. Men are 41 percent more likely than women to be caught speeding. In a recent year, 6.2 percent of male drivers were stopped for driving too fast, compared with 4.4 percent of female drivers.

GOT A FUZZ BUSTER?

At least one in 10 men between 18 and 24 uses a radar detector, as do eight percent of 25- to 34-year-old men. Blacks are more likely than white or Hispanic drivers to use the electronic devices, as are drivers of sports cars.

THINK YOU DRIVE MORE
CAREFULLY WITH A PASSENGER?

If the passenger is a woman you do. According to *Men's Car* magazine, men drive more carefully when they have a woman passenger sitting next to them, but for women it doesn't matter who else is in the car.

SWITCHED AUTO INSURANCE COMPANIES
IN THE PAST YEAR?

Ninety-four percent of drivers carry auto insurance on at least one car and 44 percent have filed a claim in the past five years. For 79 percent it was vehicle damage; for two percent, injuries; and for 19 percent both. Although eight percent of drivers have been contacted by an insurance agent or company and received a quote on auto insurance, just three percent switched their policies to a different company or agent. The Insurance Research Council says 11 percent asked friends' advice and six percent did comparative price checking.

BEEN THE DRIVER IN A CRASH RECENTLY?

Thirteen percent of men have been behind the wheel during an accident in the past five years according to the National Safe Drivers Test & Initiative Partners. Another six percent were passengers in cars that crashed. One percent were pedestrians. Another 25 percent say they've had near misses in the last 12 months, according to the Bureau of Transportation Statistics.

HOW DO YOU FEEL ABOUT "BLACK BOXES" IN CARS?

While guys appreciate how the data recorders can provide information about the details of an accident, they're reluctant to have big brother as a passenger, offering up such info as how fast they're going. According to the Insurance Research Council, they're about evenly split in supporting it. Thirty-six percent wonder if those boxes would be reliable, 16 percent fret about the cost, but 45 percent don't want anyone poking into their business.

ARE YOU LIKELIER TO BUY A TOYOTA TUNDRA OR TOYOTA RAV4?

Eighty-nine percent of Tundras are sold to men and 74 percent of RAV4 models are bought by women.

A DODGE VIPER OR STRATUS?

Ninety-one percent of Viper's sales are to men and 68 percent of both the Stratus sedan and coupe are bought by women.

THE FORD ESCAPE OR THE CHEVY SILVERADO?

While 66 percent of those who buy a Ford Escape are women, 87 percent of those clambering into the Silverado are men.

THE FORD MUSTANG OR VW BEETLE?

Tom and Ray Magliozzi, hosts of National Public Radio's *Car Talk*, consider the Ford Mustang the "ultimate guy car" and the VW Beetle in ice-cream-shop colors tops for "chicks." Women also own nearly seven of every 10 Chevrolet Cavaliers on the roads and 64 percent of Saturns. Women buy 60 to 70 percent of all small cars, and they're a lot more interested in hybrids than men are, according to J. D. Power. Men are intrigued by their technology but worry that they won't perform. True sports cars, what the industry calls "luxury models," and full-size pickups, on the other hand, have testosterone in their tanks. American men are likelier to buy an import; women are likelier to buy American.

HIGH-TECH DRIVING AIDS OR FLASHY ENTERTAINMENT SYSTEMS?

Most men want active cruise control, DVD-based navigational systems, and collision sensors—but not if it means sacrificing anything that will make the ride less fun like DVD entertainment systems or digital surround sound stereo systems. Women are more interested in collision backup sensors, night-vision systems, tire pressure monitoring, and in satellite/digital radio.

MORE INTERESTED IN THE INSIDE OR OUTSIDE OF YOUR WHEELS?

If you ask Shell for answers you'll find men are likelier to give their car a special wash and wax treatment on the outside while women are likelier to vacuum the interior and add an air freshener. A third of men would be embarrassed to drive coworkers in a filthy car; 48 percent would be humiliated if they were taking a date to dinner in a dirty car.

HOW LIKELY ARE YOU TO BUY AN ELECTRIC CAR?

Fifty-nine percent of men are happy with their gas engine and nowhere near ready to trade those in. Thirty-one percent would enjoy test-driving a hybrid however, and nine percent are ready to sign a contract.

WOULD YOU DOWNSIZE TO REDUCE FUEL USE AND AIR POLLUTION?

Assuming they're replacing the wheels that they now drive, 52 percent say they'd look at a less thirsty model. Nine percent already own or lease a small car.

INSIST ON ORIGINAL EQUIPMENT TO PATCH YOUR CAR?

Just 13 percent of male car owners would demand OEM parts rather than less costly "generic" bumpers and panels.

READ THE OWNER'S MANUAL?

Sixty-three percent of men have read bits and pieces of their owner's manual on an as-need-be basis. Eleven percent have not yet cracked the spine. Amazingly, 23 percent claim they've read it from cover to cover.

SECRETLY LONG FOR THE DAYS
WHEN THE CAR LOT WAS A MEN'S CLUB?

Sure it's politically incorrect but almost 40 percent of men secretly yearn for the days when women were seen more often there in garters and bustiers on service area pin-up calendars, draped across a car hood in promotions, or on the arm of a male customer than solo. Then her opinion, when solicited, was probably about the car color or upholstery.

10

On the Job

DO YOU LOVE YOUR JOB?

It's a veritable romance for 28 percent of men. Twenty-two percent consider it more of a friendship, although it could blossom into something more. Alas, for three percent it's been a nightmare from the get-go. A fourth of men find their company's benefits generous; 58 percent regard them as fair. Just 17 percent consider their corporate home to be way stingy.

CONSIDER YOUR WORKPLACE FAMILY?

The workplace seems more Cleaver clan than Dilbert. One in three men feel as if their colleagues are family and 45 percent, more dispassionate sorts, liken the company to a distant relative. For three out of four men, coworkers are the best part of the job. Only 18 percent avoid seeing them when they don't have to.

IRKED BY THE WAY YOUR COMPANY IS RUN?

Even if they like their company overall, they still dislike the bureaucracy and committee decision making, the glut of chiefs with too few Indians, the feedback that's never acted upon, the programs and about-faces du jour, and a management that keeps them in the dark. Overall, they're down about the low morale prevalent. Other depressants: a lack of autonomy, their boss's obnoxious personality, and a testosterone-driven culture with aggressive, rushed, short-term, risk-orientated styles of decision making.

WHAT'S THE MOST ANNOYING ASPECT OF WORK?

Surprisingly a boring mission is worse than a bad boss, men say. Being bored is the most grating aspect of a job, more disturbing than a mean manager and equipment that repeatedly breaks down, unfriendly colleagues and uncomfortable conditions. Thirty-seven percent consider their workplace a political minefield, and 40 percent describe their office as ultra PC, a place where they constantly have to watch their mouth. One in four men call their workplace filthy.

DO YOU TAKE OFF ALL THE DAYS YOU'RE ENTITLED TO?

Eighteen percent of workers don't take off all the time they're allowed. For more than two-thirds it's because of work pressure, but 10 percent enjoy work too much to be away. Others can't afford to go away, either monetarily or from fear they'll lose their job if they did.

TAKE SICK DAYS?

The average worker calls in fewer than four sick days a year with Southerners, Westerners, poor folk, and those nearing retirement or job changes taking off the most. Fifty-eight percent of workers have called in sick when they weren't. Oddly, despite their neither-snow-nor-rain motto, postal workers take the greatest number of sick days, says the Bureau of Labor Statistics. More workers call in sick on Friday than any other day of the week. Tuesday has the lowest level of absenteeism.

BEEN SICKENED BY HEALTH CARE COSTS?

In a recent year the average health premium per employee was $6,354. The typical employee pays 22 percent of that. More than half of companies have recently made changes to their plan, meaning the average Joe pays more from his own pocket when he or family members go to the doctor or drugstore.

WHAT WOULD IT TAKE FOR YOU TO PACK IT IN?

Despite protestations of loyalty and widespread "false commitment," 54 percent of workers would jump ship for a mere five to 10 percent increase in total compensation. But even if they had enough money to live comfortably for the rest of their lives, three out of four claim that they would keep on trucking.

HAS NINE-TO-FIVE BECOME SEVEN-TO-11?

Twenty-eight percent of men work late virtually every night while 35 percent put in overtime three or four nights a week. Five percent never work late. Fewer than five percent of employees work the night shift (anytime between 9:00 P.M. and 8:00 A.M.), but 23 million work outside the traditional nine to five block. Men are more likely than women to work nights.

WANT THE CORNER OFFICE?

If we'd asked that question in the dark ages of 2001, only 27 percent of guys would have demurred. Today 60 percent shudder at being CEO, according to communications consultancy Burson-Marsteller. They've heard about shortened CEO tenure and intense media scrutiny and are wary of the top job.

WRITE TO-DO LISTS
DURING MEETINGS? TAKE COFFEE BREAKS?

Without being able to doodle during meetings, how else would they ever get their personal lives in order, wonder 11 percent of men. Besides, it's one way to keep tedium at bay. More than three out of every four workers routinely take five to 15 minutes a day for a cup of joe.

IF YOU AND YOUR BOSS ARE
GOING ON THE SAME BUSINESS TRIP,
WOULD YOU SUCK UP TO HIM?

Almost two of every three men would use the occasion to get face time—aiming to book the same flight and adjacent seats, stay at the same hotel and eat together. Eighteen percent would make themselves scarce, and seven percent say they'd go out of their way to avoid the boss.

HOW OFTEN DO YOU MEET WITH YOUR BOSS?

Twelve percent meet with their boss constantly. Seventy percent get together just once every few months.

WOULD YOU FIRE YOUR BOSS IF YOU COULD?

Eighteen percent of workers would pink-slip him. Perhaps not surprisingly, those earning the least are the most eager to axe him.

WHO WOULD YOU RATHER WORK FOR?

Four out of five men would rather work for someone dumber than they are than someone who grabs the credit. The most dreaded of all bosses is the backstabber. Three out of four would rather work for a woman than someone younger than they are. They'd rather report to a demanding boss than an ill-mannered one but are torn between a mean boss and an incompetent one. Two out of three would rather work for someone who is figuratively out to lunch than an attentive meddler. And they'd rather cast their lot with a manager who's fad-oriented than a Neanderthal ostrich who believes Wite-Out defines high tech.

EVER LOST IT AT WORK?

Fewer than 20 percent of men have cried on the job (v. 60 percent of women). Nearly one in every three men has had a fight at work, most likely because someone tried to take credit for their great work or criticized it unjustly. This often prompts stealthy revenge. Thirty-four percent have gone passive aggressive, decreasing the quality of their work. Forty-six percent have contemplated changing jobs.

These Guys Do . . . Do You?

- ➤ Almost one in three men wears a uniform to work.
- ➤ Roughly 15 percent work at night. (They're unhealthier overall than the mainstream population.)
- ➤ 34 percent have lost sleep worrying about work.
- ➤ 17 percent are worried about keeping their job.
- ➤ 47 percent expect to change careers at least three times.
- ➤ 19 percent have played a joke on their boss but two out of three have censored their jokes for fear of offending a colleague.
- ➤ 53 percent dream about being their own boss.
- ➤ One in three has canceled a holiday because something has come up on the job.
- ➤ 5 percent would quit if they found out that their employer was doing something immoral, according to the Lutheran Brotherhood. Twenty-four percent have been told to do something they consider unethical. Of those, 41 percent did it.
- ➤ 72 percent want to change what they're doing now.
- ➤ Almost one in five has boomeranged—left a job and come back to the same company. (Another reason not to burn bridges.)
- ➤ 70 percent find the men they work with ruder than their female coworkers.
- ➤ 59 percent would rather have more time off than a cash bonus.
- ➤ Three out of five would rather work with a slacker than a take-over guy.
- ➤ Two out of five have stayed in a job they despised because the money was too good.

OKAY TO LET YOUR HAIR DOWN AT THE COMPANY HOLIDAY PARTY?

Unfasten it, but don't let it fly away. Fifty-seven percent of workers think flirting may be the redemption of office parties. But 18 percent warn that it's a tricky floor and very easy to slip up here. Ninety percent of men endorse mistletoe at the office bash, but of course it depends on whom they're facing that would prompt them to pucker up. Twenty-three percent of men have had morning-after regrets for their actions at the company party.

CHECK BUSINESS E-MAIL AT HOME?

About 57 percent of workers do. In fact, 42 percent dread taking time off because of the amount of e-mail awaiting them on their return.

HOW LONG DOES IT TAKE YOU TO GET TO WORK?

The average one-way commute in this country is just over 26 minutes, according to the Transportation Department. Ninety-four percent of commuters spend less than an hour getting to their job. Yet the Bureau of Transportation Statistics finds 3.3 million Americans are "stretch commuters," traveling 50 miles or more one way to their job. Nineteen percent of stretch commuters go 100 or more miles each way: 84 percent of them are men.

OFTEN CHANGE YOUR ROUTE TO WORK?

Sixteen percent of commuters change their route only when forced to do so by transportation service or weather. Just 23 percent consciously stray from their routine to liven things up.

WHERE DO YOU DO YOUR BEST WORK?

It seems not at the office desk. One in four brainstorm best in bed. Sixteen percent say lightning strikes in the shower and 14 percent get their big ideas during breaks, according to CareerEngine. Five percent find inspiration during meals. Nearly three-quarters of guys who take work home or stay home to do it feel far more productive there.

WHAT'S YOUR MOST CREATIVE/PRODUCTIVE TIME?

Morning wins by a landslide. A Creative Group survey found two-thirds call morning their most creative time. For 10 percent it's afternoon, and five percent, lunchtime/midday. Nine percent feel most creative late at night. As for the day of the week, if you want a cram feast, schedule it for Tuesday, say 48 percent of executives. Failing that, go for Monday. Most of all, avoid Friday, they warn.

MAKE YOURSELF AT HOME?

Only 19 percent of men whistle, sing, or hum while they work. Forty-nine percent regularly remove their shoes at their desk. Almost two-thirds (65 percent) listen to the radio and 28 percent keep the TV on softly when they work at home. Just three percent are neatniks. Half call their work a controlled mess. Most men are more organized at work than they are at home.

COMFORTABLE DISCUSSING POLITICS AT THE OFFICE?

Almost half of men would rather listen silently while 47 percent feel at ease chiming in. Women would much rather keep quiet during political debates than men.

LOOK AT PORN AT WORK?

Twenty-two percent of men admitted visiting a porn site while at work (v. only 12 percent of women). Of those peeping cyber-toms, 13 percent concede it was intentional.

JUNK MAIL: ELECTRONIC OR SNAIL?

By a 60/40 margin, men consider a postal mailbox full of junk mail more annoying than the 21st-century digital electronic mailbox full of junk mail.

PERSISTENT MEETINGS OR CELL PHONE RINGING?

Sixty-three percent of men would rather suffer through a work-day full of back-to-back meetings than have to listen to a cell phone that never stops ringing.

HOW LONG DO YOU EXPECT TO HUNKER DOWN?

Years ago men routinely put in 25 years toiling for a single em-ployer and walked away with a gold watch and a retirement party. Nowadays, the average guy stays on the same job for three years or less.

WORRIED ABOUT LOSING YOUR JOB?

Not as much as you might suppose. Just six percent are alarmed about the prospect with another 12 percent somewhat worried. Forty-five percent of workers have no emergency funds safety net and suspect they could get by for only four weeks without a job, according to Capital One.

FEEL APPRECIATED?

Forget about a raise: 26 percent of workers say they are seldom if ever thanked. Almost half believe they're underpaid. (On the other hand, two percent consider themselves overpaid.)

EVER ASKED FOR A RAISE?

Most are too timid but one in five men has raised his hand. (Employers respond better to men's request than they do to women's with a 59 to 45 percent success ratio.) The raise probably wasn't a barn burner, however. In a recent year the average pay hikes were just over three percent.

GOT A GUARANTEED SEVERANCE PACKAGE? A SIGN-ON BONUS?

If you're an executive you're quite likely to. More than one in three job offers made to executives included a guaranteed severance package equal to eight to 12 months of pay, says Exec-U-Net. And 40 percent of companies offer sign-up bonuses. Ditto stock options and performance-linked bonuses: 45 percent of companies offer the former to their upper-level guys and 72 percent of companies offer the latter. Forty-one percent offer performance reviews within the first six months on the job and 34 percent guarantee first-year bonuses.

WHAT'S THE MOST IMPORTANT FACTOR IN DECIDING TO TAKE A JOB?

Just as location is the mantra for home buying, salary is the trump card for 89 percent of job seekers. Still, 47 percent won't take a job they find uncreative and 39 percent would spurn one that doesn't entail sufficient responsibility. One in five considers being able to work independently a key goal.

EVER BEEN ASKED A WACKO QUESTION IN A JOB INTERVIEW?

One in five interviewees says he's been lobbed an improper or inappropriate question. Women and minorities get them more often, however, FindLaw found.

WOULD YOU RESIGN BY E-MAIL?

Only four percent of guys would sign out from cyber. One in four feels the situation requires a letter but one percent say you can get away with it by a phone call. Seventy percent feel resigning should be done in person.

EVER CHEAT ON YOUR EXPENSE ACCOUNT?

Cheating on taxes may be rampant, perhaps because it's so impersonal. Padding the expense account at work is not. Eighty-two percent of guys say they don't fudge the truth here either because it's too close to home or, in the case of 35 percent of workers, their companies scrutinize and disallow expenses.

LET YOUR INCOMING CALLS GO
DIRECTLY TO VOICE MAIL?

Some 46 percent of men say they take every call that comes in. Just four percent screen every one. The rest pick up the phone as the whim strikes. As for responding to voice mail, 42 percent ring right back as soon as they get to their desk and another 31 percent within two hours of receipt.

EVER IGNORE E-MAIL
SO THE SENDER MUST CHASE UP A RESPONSE?

E-mail senders say that on average they're forced to hound one out of every four recipients for responses. Eleven percent of e-mail recipients have falsely denied receiving an e-mail so as not to have to deal with it. Just over a third of workers reply to e-mail as soon as they receive it.

HOW OFTEN DO YOU FORGET
YOUR COMPUTER PASSWORD?

A third of men never do, but 20 percent experience such a lapse monthly or even weekly.

FEEL YOUR COMPANY IS SPYING ON YOU?

More than half of men think Big Brother is watching—and they're right. E-mail messages, phone calls, and chats in the loo are increasingly falling under corporate scrutiny. Seventy-four percent of companies do at least some surveillance: 54 percent track Internet usage and 44 percent check on phone calls. Fifteen percent use video cameras to check job performance and seven percent monitor voice-mail messages. Eighty-five percent of the spymeisters let their employees know they're being monitored.

DO YOU ALWAYS LOCK YOUR DESK AT NIGHT?

Fifty-two percent of workers with keys always use them. Four out of ten "often" lock up just to make sure, while just seven percent rarely lock anything.

EVER DATED SOMEONE FROM WORK?

Twenty-eight percent of men have gone out with a colleague. Even more have had a secret crush on one: 53 percent of single male office workers clandestinely admire a colleague. Twenty-three percent of marriage seeds were planted at work, according to the American Management Association. Only 13 percent of companies have official antiromance policies. Two out of three workplace couples initially tried to keep their relationship hush-hush.

EVER DONE "IT" AT WORK?

Forty-four percent of men say they've had sex on the job. The most popular locations: an office, a conference room, a bathroom stall, the office parking lot, and a cloakroom. Seven percent have gotten caught with their pants down and 16 percent of men have inadvertently interrupted others in the act.

EVER MAKE SEXUAL REMARKS OR INNUENDOS?

Despite the Bill O'Reilly imbroglio, 29 percent of guys have intentionally made a sly suggestion to a colleague. Thirteen per-

cent have sent a coworker cute or suggestive e-mail, and 41 percent have established prolonged eye contact. Thirty-one percent
have rubbed a colleague's shoulders. Forty-seven percent of men
would be flattered if a coworker flirted with them. At the same
time, nine percent of men are reluctant to befriend a coworker
for fear he or she might read it as an unwanted advance.

11

In the Manners Department

DO YOU BLEAT INTO YOUR CELL PHONE OBLIVIOUS OF OTHERS?

Mr. Manners you're not. Half of men say they sometimes forget they share the street (bus, train) with other people who may not want to hear their laundry list.

TURN OFF YOUR CELL PHONE AT THE MOVIES?

Forty-three percent of guys admit that they don't always power off at the movies or theater. Fifty-seven percent concede they sometimes talk during a show or movie.

HOW ABOUT CURSE LIKE A SAILOR?

Two out of five men get it off their chest no matter who's in earshot.

GIVE UP YOUR SEAT ON A
BUS FOR SOMEONE NEEDIER?

Decency, kindness, and courtesy still prevail it seems. Four out of five men say they usually give up their seat on the bus or train for a pregnant woman or elderly person.

SWITCH AIRPLANE SEATS
WHEN ANOTHER PASSENGER ASKS?

Forty-two percent of fliers feel no sense of obligation when another passenger asks them to switch seats. Five percent even consider the request rude and presumptuous. Forty-five percent will swap as long as they're improving their lot while eight percent feel good manners dictate they substitute seats whenever they are asked.

STEP ASIDE TO LET WOMEN
GET OFF THE ELEVATOR FIRST?

Maybe it's got something to do with eyeing women's bodies but three out of four men say they typically step back to allow ladies to exit the elevator before them.

OPEN THE CAR DOOR FOR THEM?

Surprisingly, in this age of sexual equality, 70 percent of men claim that they still open the car door for a woman, at least occasionally.

WHEN SOMEONE'S WAITING FOR YOUR PARKING SPOT, DO YOU HUSTLE TO VACATE IT?

Seventy-four percent feel the guy in the SUV talking on his cell phone can just cool his heels—that they like to buckle up and set the temperature and music controls before they pull out. One in four figures that common courtesy dictates that he shake a leg, as long as the motorist waiting is polite.

EVER SPIT IN PUBLIC?

Three out of five men admit that they shoot out their phlegm in public. (Far fewer women do, or at least say that they do.) Then again, 41 percent of guys confess that they have burped and farted in public without apology.

WHEN YOU HAVE TO BURP IN COMPANY . . . WHAT TO DO?

A third of men say that when the power manifests itself, they simply let it rip. That's more than the number who would excuse themselves and go to another room, or who would do the deed and then apologize.

DRIVE LIKE A MANIAC?

More than one in every three guys admits he sometimes (okay, often) is rude and ruthless when behind the wheel.

HOW OFTEN DO YOU JUMP THE LINE?

Wheels or feet, it doesn't matter: one in four guys considers cutting the line part of the game. Interestingly, more than three out of four will protest when they're the ones victimized.

ALWAYS SAY PLEASE AND THANK YOU?

More than one in three men—36 percent—say they almost always practice these courtesies while 48 percent sometimes do. Sixteen percent admit it wouldn't hurt them to mutter these pleasantries more often.

SLURP YOUR SOUP? CHEW WITH YOUR MOUTH OPEN? GRAB AND RUN?

Table manners are not men's strong suit. One in three often slurps his soup; 27 percent "probably" eat with their mouth open, and 86 percent often plant their elbows on the table. Four out of five men consider the dining table to be an each man (woman and child) for himself zone.

COUGH OR SNEEZE WITHOUT COVERING YOUR MOUTH?

One in three men (34 percent) admits he has spewed his germs into the air with no attempt to confine them.

DO YOU ALWAYS FLUSH?

That depends on what has been deposited. If it's yellow, at least one in four guys will let it mellow. When it's brown, almost all flush it down. Overall, 24 percent of men admit that they don't *always* remember to flush.

HOW ABOUT PUT THE TOILET SEAT DOWN AFTER YOU'VE PEED?

Forty-seven percent of men swear that they always put the seat down after they've used the john. (Women who *always* find it up are skeptical about that.)

HOG THE JOHN?

Nearly three out of four men (71 percent) admit to reading on the toilet (vs. 56 percent of women). Magazines are the reading material of choice followed by newspapers for the gents (and books for ladies). The least-preferred reading material in the john: the mail.

ASK BEFORE TAKING THE LAST HELPING OF FOOD, OR GRAB IT?

That depends on where you're eating. If you're with the guys, it's love and war—all's fair and each man for himself. If you're in mixed company, a kinder, gentler set of manners apply.

DO YOU WRITE THANK-YOU NOTES?

While two out of three women write thank-you notes when the occasion warrants it, just 41 percent of men are likely to put pen to paper or fingers to keyboard to express their gratitude.

RECLINE YOUR SEAT IN A PLANE IF THERE'S SOMEONE BEHIND YOU?

One in three travelers does so and doesn't consider it rude. Twenty -one percent regard that as bad form and 46 percent okay it if it's not pushed back all the way. Nearly half of fliers, however, admit they put the seat back all the way, on almost every flight.

ADDRESS PEOPLE BY COURTESY TITLES LIKE MR. OR MS.?

Assuming it's someone you don't know who is older or eminent, 63 percent of men say they use this more formal address almost all the time.

BARGE IN TO OTHERS' CONVERSATIONS?

Four out of five guys admit they sometimes interrupt others or speak out of turn.

HONK YOUR CAR HORN IN IRRITATION?

Even in so-called quiet zones, 69 percent of men say they've leaned on their horn.

UP ON YOUR NETIQUETTE?

Yahoo! found guys sorely lacking in Internet decorum. One in three occasionally types in CAPITAL LETTERS, the equivalent of shouting in e-mail, and even more are guilty of acronym overuse and "spamming" friends by forwarding them jokes, video, and chain letters. Unlike women, however, they usually fill in the subject line and avoid excessive punctuation!!!

12

In the Kitchen, at the Supermarket, in a Restaurant, and Around the Dinner Table

Kitchen Confidential

CAN YOU COOK?

Maybe you're no Wolfgang Puck but 57 percent of men think they're pretty good at the burners. Thirteen percent consider themselves "accomplished." On the other hand, 16 percent moan that all they can do in the kitchen is boil an egg or make toast.

ENJOY IT?

Thirteen percent of men liken preparing dinner to creating a work of art. Fourteen percent consider it akin to going to the dentist—something they dread.

WHO TAUGHT YOU HOW TO COOK?

Three out of four children credit their mother with teaching them their way around the kitchen. In 29 percent of families, the father has been the prime instructor.

KNOW WHICH KNIFE TO USE TO CHOP CELERY, ONIONS, AND CARROTS?

Seventy-six percent of men know to use a chef's knife, not a paring or a serrated knife for this task. (Just 70 percent of women know that.)

WHAT ARE THE MEALS YOU'RE ABSOLUTELY SECURE MAKING?

A spaghetti dinner, meaning pasta with jarred sauce, is one of five foods the average nonculinary-minded man feels confident preparing. The others are frozen pizza, scrambled eggs, baked potatoes, and tossed green salad.

ARE YOU THE BARBECUER?

Two out of three times, it's the guy who wears the toque outdoors—even if she decides what to grill. Sixty percent of guys do it on a charcoal grill, and 63 percent of them marinate before grilling. Men are more likely to go for bold and spicy barbecue sauce than women who tend to prefer sweeter sauces. Men eat more grilled food than women do—23.7 pounds a year to 20.5 for women. Steak is their top choice. (For women steak is tied with chicken).

WHAT'S IN YOUR FRIDGE?

Glad Products and Whirlpool have peeked inside men's refrigerator to find it's they who have the sweeter tooth. While 60 percent of both genders keep ice cream on hand, men more often have candy bars and cake there as well. And while 61 percent of women keep bottled water in the refrigerator, only 48 percent of men do. Beer is found in close to 42 percent of men's refrigerators. Ninety-three percent of fridges of both genders have leftover takeout. More than half of guys complain they have a hard time finding items in their refrigerator because it's overcrowded.

DO YOU THROW AWAY MILK
WHEN IT REACHES THE EXPIRATION DATE?

The date on the carton is just the date after which it can't be sold. The milk probably has another week of freshness to go. Sour milk may not taste good but it won't do you any harm. Forty percent of men know that.

WHEN COOKING A
FROZEN PIZZA, DO YOU JAZZ IT UP?

Two out of three guys sometimes or often pop a pizza in the oven, but just 22 percent rip open the package, bake and take it as it comes. The rest adjust the sausage and pepperoni, rearrange the cheese, or add anchovies or other toppings.

At the Supermarket

Eighty-five percent of men are in the grocery store at least once a month and 36 percent claim to be the prime shopper in their families.

DO YOU TAKE THE FIRST MILK IN THE DAIRY CASE?

Almost three of every four men reach behind the front milk in the freezer case to take a fresher carton. Midwesterners are least likely to do so, but even they pay attention to freshness dating.

WHEN PICKING ROLLS OR PASTRIES, DO YOU USE THE TONGS?

Nine out of 10 male shoppers pick out their rolls or pastries with their hands.

WHEN YOU DON'T WANT SOMETHING IN YOUR CART, WHERE DO YOU DITCH IT?

Assuming it's not something from the freezer, 45 percent of guys put it wherever they are when they realize they don't want it. Just over five percent of men feel some shame about this and try to cover over the crime. The rest either leave it at the check-out counter or bring it back to its rightful place.

MUNCH ON THE FREE SAMPLES OFFERED?

Four out of five men take advantage of the freebie demonstration foods served up in the supermarket. And one in four nibbles on whatever catches his fancy that's available to buy—whether the store is offering it to sample or not.

GO ON THE FAST LANE WITH MORE THAN THE LIMIT OF ITEMS?

One in every four guys sneaks onto the express lane with one or two more items than specified and 10 percent try to slip by five or more items above the posted limit.

USE A SHOPPING LIST? COUPONS?

Almost nine in 10 men take a shopping list to the store but fewer than one in three sticks to it faithfully. Three out of four men use coupons, although only one in four uses them every time he food shops. Just one in five says his coupons are neatly organized.

FIND GROCERY SHOPPING FUN?

Just about 15 percent of men feel they were born to grocery shop. Another 16 percent live to beat the system through coupons and sales.

Eating Out

PASSED THROUGH THE GOLDEN ARCHES?

Sixty percent of men have dined at McDonald's in the last month and 48 percent have been to a Burger King.

USUALLY BRING HOME
LEFTOVERS FROM A DINNER OUT?

Fifty-six percent of the time men eat at a restaurant they take home a doggie bag (v. 67 percent of the time for women). However, more men (91 percent) than women (86 percent) are likely to actually eat those restaurant leftovers.

ASSUME MONEY'S NO OBJECT:
WHAT WOULD YOU ORDER?

Steak remains the first choice for men, with medium as the degree of doneness requested most often. Men are 20 percent more likely than women to use steak sauce. Hands down, more people order French fries at a restaurant than any other food. Twenty-two percent of all restaurant meals include them.

WHEN YOU MUST LEAVE YOUR NAME
ON A RES, DO YOU LEAVE YOUR REAL ONE?

Thirty percent of guys making a reservation leave a fake name to secure a table. The longest the average guy will wait at the bar before going someplace else is half an hour.

EVER SEND FOOD BACK?

No matter that the burger is well done and he specified rare, 34 percent won't send it back.

HOW ABOUT ASK FOR A DIFFERENT TABLE?

If seated next to the john, kitchen, or swinging doors, roughly two out of three men would ask for a different table. The rest are too timid to speak up—or oblivious of the atmosphere.

WHAT'S YOUR FAVORITE DINER FOOD?

Burger and fries wins with meat loaf running a close second. Other favorites among men: bacon and eggs, macaroni and cheese, and pie and rice pudding.

AS SOMEONE'S GUEST, DO YOU SCRIMP OR SPLURGE?

Most men play the middle card, opting for a choice in the middle range. Thirteen percent would order one of the cheaper entrees and 18 percent would order whatever they wanted, no matter what it cost.

DO YOU STUDY THE BILL?

More than half of guys (51 percent) give it a cursory glance and will only pore over it if the figure seems widely out of whack. Forty-three percent hand over their credit card or money with just a quick look. Six percent scrutinize the check, eager to find an error and tell the waiter about it.

EVER ASK FOR STUFF OFF THE MENU?

Seventy-one percent of men either ask for something not on the menu but which they know the chef regularly prepares, or ask the waiter to modify the dish by omitting the capers or anchovies, say.

USUALLY ORDER DESSERT IN A RESTAURANT?

Men are far likelier than women—particularly coastal ones—to order dessert. But they're far less likely to request raspberries or strawberries, which would brand them as wimps.

COMFORTABLE COMING OUT WITH THE RIGHT TIP?

A third of men have this down pat. They know to double the tax or do some other quickie math. Trouble comes determining what to leave the captain or wine steward.

Chowing Down

WHAT ARE YOUR MAINSTAYS?

The typical man eats 78 pounds of chicken a year, a tad over 50 pounds of pork, 15.6 pounds of fish (v. 37.4 pounds for Europeans and 88 pounds for Japanese), and 23 pounds of pizza.

HOW LIKELY ARE YOU TO TRY NEW FOODS?

While few men are still into three squares a day, just 14 percent claim to be very adventurous eaters. Another 14 percent enjoy the reliability of eating the same thing every day, but 65 percent figure that would get boring awfully fast. One in five usually eats the same thing for lunch (or another meal), but that's because there's little choice. Just one in 10 is open to trying chitlins.

HOW ABOUT TOFU?

In early 1980 the Trader Vic's restaurant in San Francisco published a table flyer and wall poster where an Asian beauty offers to "Put a Little Tofu in Your Life." Several restaurants and delis began substituting it in salads, sandwiches, burgers, pizzas, soups, blintzes, and lasagna. But it still retains that quichelike new-man image. Despite its healthful attributes, just 18 percent of men claim to knowingly ever eat tofu.

BINGE ON BACON?

Real men may have balked at quiche but never had a problem with bacon. According to NPDFoodworld, the traditional breakfast of eggs, bacon, and sausage is making a comeback, with recent sales the highest they've been in 10 years.

HOW DO YOU DE-SHELL YOUR PEANUTS?

Ninety-six percent of guys eat nuts and pistachios with seven percent not bothering to remove the shell. Twelve percent buy them preshelled. Three out of four shell and eat each one at a time while two percent prepare a whole batch to enjoy . . . and then toss them down the hatch.

WOULD YOU EAT LESS TO BE GUARANTEED TO LIVE LONGER?

There's a reason they say that the way to a man's heart is through his stomach. Seventy percent of men would refuse to cut calories to add years. For that matter, only 40 percent of men want to live past 100.

WHAT WOULD YOU ASK FOR, FOR A LAST MEAL?

Maybe this will give you a clue: more death-row inmates ask for French fries over anything else, followed by hamburgers, T-bone steak, and fried chicken, with ice cream for dessert.

INTO CHOCOLATE?

More than twice as many men (40 percent) as women (20 percent) buy chocolate for others, instead of themselves. But while half of women hide their chocolate, 73 percent of men would never even consider that. Many more women than men feel guilty about eating chocolate (86 v. 65 percent). Women, however, take smaller bites, nibbling rather than wolfing chocolate, by a two-to-one margin.

DRINK COFFEE?

Seventy-three percent of guys do. Five percent even have four or five cups a day. More take it black than any other way but if they use a creamer, they prefer whole milk to skim.

DO YOU DUNK OR COAT YOUR FOOD IN KETCHUP?

Assuming you're a ketchup lover (and who isn't?) 36 percent of men and 29 percent of women coat their food with the stuff poured directly from the bottle. Women prefer to dunk as it controls the amount of ketchup released. They're also much more likely to use mayonnaise than men are, whereas men tend to use and enjoy barbecue sauce more than women.

WOULD YOU EAT SOMETHING DREADFUL FOR A BIG PAYOUT?

Ten percent of guys say they would eat a rat or an insect on a re-ality TV show. More would opt to bungee jump from a high bridge or be covered in spiders than to eat a plate of maggots. Only eight percent could contemplate such a repast.

IF IT FALLS ON THE FLOOR, WOULD YOU EAT IT ANYWAY?

Some 56 percent of men (and 70 percent of women) live by the five-second rule.

WHAT TIME DO YOU
USUALLY EAT DINNER?

The most popular time seems to be 6:00–6:30 P.M. with 35 percent of us at the table then. Another 26 percent usually eat early (4:00–5:30 P.M.) and 22 percent from 7:00–7:30 P.M. The rest usually eat later.

GOT A THING FOR SALT?

Experts recommend guys have 3.8 grams of salt a day—something like two-thirds of a teaspoon. The average Joe takes in more than twice that—7.8 to 11.8 grams of salt each day, not counting what they sprinkle on at the table. (The average woman ingests 5.8 to 7.8 grams.)

WHAT TICKLES YOUR TASTE BUDS?

When forced to select just one flavor, garlic trumps runners-up: onion, mesquite/BBQ, spicy, and citrus. Young men from the South or the West buy most of the hot sauce sold.

EAT QUICHE?

Real men still don't, at least not by choice. Fewer than one in four would order it in a restaurant and fewer than one in 10 includes it among his favorites.

GIVE UP SEX OR YOUR FAVORITE FOOD?

Perhaps the way to a man's heart is not through his stomach after all. Ninety-one percent of men would ditch the food; just seven percent would forfeit sex.

PICKLES: SWEET OR SOUR?

Men widely prefer dill (or sour) pickles to sweet ones and they're likelier to call a long sandwich with cold cuts, cheese, and lettuce a "sub" rather than a "hoagie" or "hero."

HOW OFTEN DO YOU SNACK?

Some 73 percent of men go at it at least once a day. Thirty-nine percent nosh more than twice daily while just four percent insist they never snack at all. Men are more likely than women to snack because they're hungry; women are more likely than men to snack out of boredom.

CONSIDER FRENCH FRIES A FRESH VEGETABLE?

Even with these lard-encrusted starch sticks dressed in battered coats, 15 percent of men consider them vegetables.

HOW DO YOU EAT AN OREO?

Half of all Oreo eaters pull them apart. Men are far likelier than women to eat them intact (84 percent v. 49 percent).

SEPARATE YOUR FOOD?

While not obsessive about them touching, three out of five men keep the rice apart from the meat. And one out of every three of them eats in a distinct order, either all of one offering first or in a fixed pattern.

DO YOU EAT CORN ON THE COB ROW BY ROW?

Fifty-eight percent approach this like a math problem and attack the maize row by row. Just 36 percent eat corn randomly.

At the Bar

INTO BEER?

Twenty-three percent of guys drink beer on a regular basis. For almost all beer was the first alcoholic beverage they tried. Eighteen percent most often drink liquor and 45 percent, wine. The rest divide their alcoholic appetite somewhat evenly. Fourteen percent of men admit that they sometimes drink more than they should and 31 percent confess that drinking has been a cause of trouble in their family.

KNOW WINES?

Sixty percent of men feel confident when it comes to choosing a quality bottle of wine. Only five percent are sufficiently adept to call themselves an oenophile. Fifty-three percent avoid the wine list if they can fob it off on someone else.

PREFER RED OR WHITE WINE?

Forty-four percent of adults overall prefer red wine, but 57 percent of men do, according to Vinexpo Americas. Although the admonition to drink red wine with meat and white with chicken and fish is purely aesthetic—and meant to be broken—half of men believe it's a cardinal rule.

GOT A SET AGENDA WHEN YOU WALK INTO A WINE STORE?

Men tend to look for a specific wine that has a good rating from a magazine. They care about whose cellar is biggest. Women on the other hand often come into a store with a friend's recommendation and are open to something else. Women ask questions; men as a rule think they should know the answers already so they bluff.

USUALLY DRINK A NIGHTCAP BEFORE BED?

Thirteen percent of men regard a nightcap as a pre-bedtime ritual. On the other hand, 38 percent are teetotalers. Of those who do drink, one in four rarely indulges.

13

At Home

A PLACE TO CRASH OR REFLECTION OF YOU?

Three out of four men (77 percent) say that their homes are mirrors of themselves. Eighty-two percent think it's a better long-term investment than the stock market.

GOT A MAN CAVE?

Not if you're in a relationship you don't. But 29 percent of bachelors keep weight sets and foosball tables on full display at all times nearby their ready-to-assemble entertainment center, pair of leather reclining chairs, and big-screen TV.

YOU DO THE DECORATING?

A man's home may be his castle, but if he's got a woman in his life chances are from the blenders to balustrades, cookware to curtains, wing chairs to wainscoting, she's furnishing the king-dom. On the other hand, men buy the vacuum cleaners so they're sold by their amperage or raw power—because market research says male shoppers want "maximum suck."

RATHER HAVE AN IN-GROUND POOL OR A POSH HOME THEATER?

Thirty-eight percent would rather swim, but 49 percent would rather watch movies. For the rest, neither pleasure is to be slighted. Almost half of men—45 percent—already have a home theater space, most likely located in the family room or den.

RATHER HAVE YOUR GARAGE REORGANIZED OR HOUSE PAINTED?

Not every man is a power tool type but still, 29 percent would rather have someone reorganize his garage rather than paint the exterior of his house, clean out the rain gutters or put in a new gutter system, or install a new fence in his yard.

PERFECT INTERIOR DECOR OR A PERFECTLY LANDSCAPED YARD?

Fifty-one percent of men would rather have a home with perfect interior decor. Just 18 percent would rather have a perfectly landscaped yard.

WHAT WOULD YOU LIKE TO SEE ADDED ON TO YOUR HOME?

More men opt for a pond or some other "water feature" or a deck than go for a pool or patio. Ten percent would like to add a garden.

WANT MORE SPACE?

New houses have increased in size 24 percent to 2,080 square feet since 1985, and new homes are being built with an average of 2,200 square feet, but only 10 percent of men say they need more living space. Nineteen percent would actually rather live in a smaller house.

TRADITIONAL OR MODERN FURNITURE?

Men prefer a look they can relate to—meaning tradition trumps avant-garde. Most men prefer neutral tones. It's no secret why men and their furniture get a bad rap as deficient home decorators. A recent survey by the American Furniture Manufacturers Association to determine guys' preferences and attitudes found that men favor beds, recliners, and sofas. Sixteen percent of (mostly younger) men admit they exist in sparse spaces with no more than a patio chair and a really big TV.

NEW STUFF?

Although 18 percent of men expect to buy some new furniture within the next year or two, few are enthusiastic about the process. According to the American Furniture Manufacturers Association, while more than three out of four women really love to shop for furniture, 74 percent of men would rather do virtually anything else.

GOT A FAVORITE CHAIR?

Archie Bunker knew whereof he sat. Ninety-four percent of men say they've got a favorite chair. Many go for the La-Z-Boy style.

WHAT'S YOUR FAVORITE
COLOR SCHEME AT HOME?

Paint it blue. That has always been men's favorite color and it still is. Their second favorite decorating color is green. Least appealing: orange and chartreuse, yellow and indigo. The top three colors for the bathroom: sky blue, pale apricot, and royal blue. After white, yellow is men's favorite color in the kitchen. Blue is also men's favorite color toothbrush but surprisingly lilac comes in second.

BLACK SHEETS?

Twenty-six percent of men say they're tempted and 21 percent have already bought black sheets. (Oddly, twice as many men who call themselves Democrats as Republicans claim to have bought black.)

GO BAREFOOT?

Sixty-two percent of men almost always shuffle around the house barefoot with four percent preferring to keep on socks. Just 10 percent rarely if ever trudge around their homes barefoot.

PUT YOUR FEET UP ON THE COFFEE TABLE?

You mean, some guys don't? While 15 percent of men claim they like their furniture too much to possibly scuff it, five percent say furniture that has a lived-in look is preferable to any other kind. Forty-five percent make sure they don't have shoes on when they put up their feet.

SET UP YOUR OWN SOUND SYSTEM?

Even if it isn't plug and play, 77 percent of men say they set up their own consumer electronics.

WHAT'S YOUR FAVORITE ROOM IN THE HOUSE?

The old adage "No matter where I serve my guests they seem to like my kitchen best" apparently rings true. DDB Needham Worldwide found that 28 percent of men (and 48 percent of women) like to hang out best near the old cooker. In fact, research shows the average guy turns on the faucet 16 times a day and goes through 168 gallons of water daily.

WHAT'S THE MOST IMPORTANT ROOM IN THE HOUSE?

Fifty-four percent of men consider the living or family room as the most important space in the home, and 23 percent vote for the kitchen. Only three percent select the dining room, yet few use it except for special occasions.

14

Among Gadgets

ARE YOU A TECHNO GEEK?

Almost half of all men admit they've got gadget envy—an almost insatiable need for the latest techno-doodad. Forty-two percent want to know about home entertainment products as soon as they come out. While few sufferers of what's jocularly been called "male pattern gearness" actualize their daydreams, marketers of this stuff have made liberal use of men's yearning.

SO WHAT'S ON YOUR WISH LIST?

Leading it are plasma televisions and computers followed by HDTV, digital cameras, and DVD players. Men are also interested in gadgets to e-mail photos and burn audio CDs, watch DVDs on PCs, and purchase or download MP3 files. Almost half of men (46 percent) would love a home theater (v. fewer than one in every three women) and most want it to be obtrusive. Forty percent of men would agree to watch chick flicks and one in 10 say they'd even jump out of an airplane for their big-screen TV, if you consider Circuit City a credible source. But 43 percent are wary of buying one because they are so bulky. Still, 51 percent admit to envying friends who have bigger TV sets than theirs.

CAN YOU EXPLAIN AN MP3 PLAYER TO A FRIEND?

Four out of 10 guys say they're up on MP3 players and 35 percent can describe how they work. Far fewer own an iPod.

EXPECT TO SWAP OUT YOUR LANDLINE FOR JUST THE CELL PHONE?

Some six percent of men expect to have cut the cord within the next year and another seven percent are mulling it.

KNOW HOW TO USE EVERYTHING ON YOUR CELL PHONE?

Almost half—47 percent—of wireless subscribers don't know how to use all of their phone's features and functions.

HOW OFTEN DO YOU CHANGE THE RING TONE ON YOUR CELL PHONE?

While most men never or rarely do, 23 percent claim to change that tune weekly. Twice as many guys have a polyphonic preset ring as have anything else, but the next most popular is a TV or movie theme song. That slightly edges out the percent of men who have beeps, which trumps the number who have buzzes, which tops the percent who've personalized their own noise.

USE ALL THE TIME ON
YOUR WIRELESS PLAN EACH MONTH?

Half of wireless subscribers said they use fewer minutes each month than their plan allows, while only 10 percent often exceed their monthly limit. Thirteen percent use more than 1,000 minutes a month.

EVER LOOK YOURSELF UP
ON A SEARCH ENGINE?

Ever? Thirty-nine percent of men admit they've tried to find themselves on Google or other search engines. Thirty-six percent say they've searched for friends they have lost touch with and 29 percent looked up a family member. Seventeen percent have searched for an ex-girlfriend. Men were more likely than women to look up automobiles and technology and science topics and women were more likely than men to search for information on health and fashion as well as celebrity news and scandals.

HOW ARE YOU CONNECTED?

For home Internet connection a third have a modem, 3.3 percent use ISDN, and 24.3 percent, XDSL while 35.8 percent have a cable connection and 1.3 percent go wireless. One percent have a satellite connection. While 73 percent of working men have access to a high-speed Internet connection on the job, only a third have a high-speed connection at home.

HOW MANY E-MAIL ADDRESSES
DO YOU CURRENTLY HAVE?

Just one in five men has only one sign-on. Twenty-nine percent have two (one for work and one for pleasure) and 22 percent have three. Perhaps to accommodate nefarious ends, 12 percent have four and 18 percent have even more.

Whatcha Got?

> - Some 36 percent have a carbon monoxide detector.
> - 69 percent own a DVD player.
> - 81 percent own a cordless phone.
> - 22 percent own an MPS player (v. 12 percent of women).
> - 56 percent have a modem.
> - 7 percent own and use a Web camera.
> - 20 percent have an electric toothbrush.
> - 51 percent have a digital TV.
> - 14 percent use a wireless device like a Blackberry or Palm Pilot.
> - 7 percent have a TIVO or digital TV recorder clone although 16 percent think they own one.
> - 82 percent have an answering machine.
> - 14 percent own a water filter.
> - 27 percent have a pager or beeper.
> - 40 percent have caller ID.
> - 68 percent own a cell phone.
> - 36 percent own a chain saw.
> - 58 percent have a TV in their bedroom.
> - 71 percent have a spyware detector or removal program installed on their computer.
> - 34 percent have a computer that is less than a year old.
> - 95 percent have a toolbox at home.
> - 26 percent have installed a firewall in their computers.

➤ More men currently have a bulky cathode-ray tube
monitor for their desktop computer but not for long. In
2004 sales of the slick, svelte liquid-crystal displays
nudged past CRT displays.

WHATCHA WANT? SUBWOOFER?

For one in every three guys (but one in seven percent of women)
this is a big deal.

IN A PDA?

Most men want their handheld computers to be compatible with
their Outlook e-mail programs and to have wireless capability.
Women, on the other hand, look to their PDA to give them access to directions and maps while driving.

HOW IMPORTANT IS IT THAT
THE ELECTRONICS BE EASY TO USE?

For most gals, it's critical, but for guys it's far less important. For
them, product quality or performance is chief followed by features and then price.

WHO CONTROLS THE REMOTE?

In a Woody Allen classic, the son asks his father who's the boss
in their family. The affronted dad sputters that he is—that mom
makes the decisions but he controls the TV channel switcher.
There are more remote controls in America than there are people. The average home has more than four. Only seven percent
rarely use them. With so many remotes, 68 percent of guys

admit they're often befuddled figuring out which remote belongs to which electronic device. Rather than go without a remote, 60 percent of guys have "borrowed" the batteries from another appliance to keep that one running. Magnavox found twice as many women as men would rather give up sex than their domination of the TV remote control for one week.

It Takes a Man Around the House

WHATCHA DO? DOES DIY MEAN "DO IT YOURSELF" OR "DECIDE IT YOURSELF"?

While 71 percent of men claim they're very confident they would know how to fix something around the house (v. just 58 percent of women), 76 percent consider themselves do-it-yourselfers (even if they don't quite get around to the doing part). Half of men plan to do something to their home in the next year or two—and 60 percent of home owners—but more of them will get the work done without the sweat of their own brow.

DEFENDED YOUR HOME AGAINST A TERRORIST ATTACK?

Fifty-two percent of men have followed former Homeland Security Advisor Tom Ridge's admonition to stock up on duct tape. Forty-one percent have made plans to evacuate from their homes in the event of a terrorist attack, natural disaster, or other crisis.

WHICH ROOM GETS THE MOST ATTENTION?

For men refurnishing or redecorating, it's the master bedroom that gets the most attention followed by the living room, bathroom, and then kitchen and dining room. If they're paying for renovation, kitchens top the list followed by bathrooms.

CHECKED THE SMOKE DETECTOR RECENTLY?

Eighty-five percent have checked the batteries in their smoke alarms and/or carbon monoxide detectors within the past 18 months. Most do it during daylight saving time.

WHEN ASSEMBLING SOMETHING, DO YOU FOLLOW THE INSTRUCTIONS?

Most guys wing it: just 37 percent say they always let the instructions be their guide. Fifty-three percent admit they don't always follow the instructions exactly, yet alone read them. Eight percent rely strictly on intuition.

KEEP THE USER GUIDES FOR YOUR MAJOR APPLIANCES?

More than nine in every 10 men (92 percent) keep the instruction manuals and 76 percent file records of major home repairs. Three out of four have money set aside ostensibly for emergency home repairs. But just 52 percent keep basic maintenance or home repair books around.

WHAT COULD YOU DO?

More than nine out of ten men (94 percent) say they could hang a mirror or artwork using a wall anchor, and 84 percent swear that they could fix a leaky faucet. More than three out of four (78 percent) confirm that they could change an electrical outlet—the same number who could hang a fixture. Three out of four say they could (not would but could) wallpaper a room, and the same number could fix a hole in a wall.

HOW DO YOU FEEL ABOUT FIXING THAT HOLE IN THE CEILING?

You may not like that hole in the roof where the rain comes in but getting around to fixing it is another matter. Most guys say that home improvement projects are not what they live for. It ranks above visiting their spouse's or partner's family and shopping for shoes with their spouse or partner as a favorite weekend activity, but considerably below exercising or playing sports and watching TV.

HOW'D YOU LEARN TO BE MR. FIX-IT?

More men say they taught themselves than credit any other teacher. In second place, their dad. Four percent claim they learned what they know from their spouse.

WHAT'S THE MOST INDISPENSABLE TOOL FROM YOUR TOOL KIT?

The screwdriver wins hands down (32 percent), easily surpassing the drill (19 percent), hammer (18 percent), and pliers (12 percent). Down in single digits are the wrench (eight percent), circular saw (six percent), handsaw (two percent), and sander (less than one percent).

USUALLY TACKLE MINOR REPAIRS AND SPRUCE-UPS ON YOUR OWN?

In the last year, 86 percent of guys have worked on small do-it-yourself home improvement projects like painting, fixing faucets, and replacing hardware. Forty-seven percent say they attempt minor plumbing repairs and 44 percent, minor electrical repairs.

EVER INSTALL A NEW TOILET YOURSELF?

One in every five guys has tackled this task, according to Kohler.

HOW ABOUT THE BIG JOBS?

In the last year, 38 percent of guys have worked on a large do-it-yourself home improvement project like building a deck, replacing windows, or remodeling the kitchen or bathroom. (Just 24 percent of women are so inclined.)

FOR WHAT DO YOU CALL IN THE PROS?

Just over half (52 percent) hire someone else to paint the interior of their home and 64 percent pay for a pro to paint the outside. Only 11 percent will take a crack at major plumbing repairs.

EVER RAID ANOTHER FIXTURE TO REPLACE A BURNED-OUT BULB?

Six in 10 men admit they have borrowed from Peter to pay Paul, so to speak.

HOW LONG DO YOU WAIT
TO CHANGE A BURNED-OUT BULB?

One in three drops everything and gets to it immediately—while one in three puts it out of his mind for a few days, perhaps hoping someone else will replace it. One in five changes it fast but when he has time. Fourteen percent say they try to duck out of this as often as possible.

Maintenance Man

DO YOU ROUTINELY EMPTY
THE TRASH BEFORE IT'S FULL?

Two out of three men wait until the garbage seriously needs to be emptied. Fifty-six percent recycle and 56 percent usually rinse out cans/bottles/containers before tossing.

DO YOU ALWAYS LOCK UP
AS A PRE-BEDTIME RITUAL?

Some 59 percent of guys say they routinely go around locking doors to their house or apartment before going to sleep. One in four religiously turns off the lights when he leaves a room.

ARE YOU A CLEANLINESS COMPULSIVE?

There are a lot of Lad Macbeths out there. Only 12 percent have ever turned their clothes inside out to avoid doing laundry and almost half claim to change their towels after every shower. Most men change the sheets once a week and 46 percent make their bed every day (v. 76 percent of women). On the other hand, most men let their magazines swell into skyscrapers and only 13 percent alphabetize or organize their books and CDs.

WHAT IS YOUR MOST
DREADED HOUSEHOLD CHORE?

More men find cleaning the bathroom the worst straw to draw. Washing the dishes is second. Men would much rather mop the floors, fix the car, or cook. Ten percent of men have never done a load of laundry.

USUALLY GET SPRING (CLEANING) FEVER?

Big surprise: men are less likely than women to be seasonally motivated: just 35 percent are. But then women are the home's primary sanitation engineer—good job of passing the buck on that one. They are, however, none too happy about it.

15

Out of this World (Spiritually Speaking)

DO YOU BELIEVE IN GOD?

Eighty-six percent of men in America do (compared to 93 percent of women). More than half don't look kindly on atheists and only 32 percent think that nonbelievers can get into heaven. Recently, however, their view of God has been changing. Only 63 percent of men believe God is the all-knowing, all-powerful Heavenly Father who can be reached by prayer (v. 73 percent of women) while 17 percent see him as an idea, not a being. Nine percent imagine God as an impersonal creator. Two out of three men believe that all people are called before God on Judgment Day to answer for their sins. Many more think of God as a judge than as a lover.

DO YOU BELIEVE IN MIRACLES?

Four out of five people do, with men somewhat less likely than women counting themselves as believers.

THINK THAT GOD HELPS THOSE WHO HELP THEMSELVES?

Although their creedal understandings are sometimes vague, 81 percent of men believe in a Supreme Being who helps those who help themselves; only 17 percent dismiss the slogan as word-smithing.

DO YOU BELIEVE IN HEAVEN?

More than eight out of 10 adults do. They include 89 percent of women but only 75 percent of men, and just 71 percent of those aged 25 to 29 and those with postgraduate degrees.

DO YOU ENVISION HEAVEN AS A REAL PLACE WITH HARPS ET AL?

Forty-three percent expect to find harps and angels once they pass through the pearly gates. At the same time, 69 percent believe in angels.

AND HELL?

Sixty-five percent of men (and 73 percent of women) believe in the devil's lair. Two out of three of those convinced of brimstone conceive of it as an actual place where people who have led bad lives without being sorry are eternally damned, instead of as an idea. Thirty-eight percent personally know someone who they think will end up there.

EXPECT TO GO TO HEAVEN?

Some 31 percent of men feel they've got an excellent shot at passing through the pearly portals. Another 41 percent consider their chances pretty good.

HOW ABOUT THAT OTHER PLACE?

Just two percent feel they don't stand a prayer of getting into that upstairs gated community because they're surely headed in the opposite direction. Twenty-two percent of guys admit that worry about where they're ultimately going ambushes them.

THINK GOD CREATED THE EARTH IN SIX DAYS?

Three out of five guys (61 percent) think the biblical tale of creation is "literally true." Sixty percent also totally accept the story of Noah's ark as fact and 64 percent believe Moses parted the Red Sea.

CONSIDER THE BIBLE THE ACTUAL WORD OF GOD?

Forty percent of men say it's to be taken literally, word for word, while 42 percent believe that while it's the word of God, not everything in it should be taken literally, word for word. Thirteen percent feel the Bible is a book written by men and is not the word of God.

DO YOU ACTUALLY READ THE BIBLE?

Last year, 59 percent of Americans dipped into the Big Book at least occasionally. Twenty years earlier, three out of four were doing so more or less regularly. One reason fewer pages are being turned is that church attendance is down. While more than four in 10 Americans say they attended a church or synagogue in the past week, 61 percent of those in the pews were women.

BELIEVE MEDIUMS CAN COMMUNICATE WITH THE DEAD?

People like John Edward and James Van Praagh are sought after because 28 percent of guys believe certain people can connect with spirits and hear their messages. That's up from 18 percent a decade ago.

DO YOU BELIEVE THAT IMPLORING THE ALMIGHTY PAYS OFF?

Thirty percent of Americans think that if they ask God for something and they behave well, they'll get what they asked for. Four out of five say they have thanked God for their financial well-being while seven out of 10 consider their financial situation to be a reflection of God's regard for them.

HOW SUPERSTITIOUS ARE YOU?

Fifty-nine percent of guys would walk under a ladder, step on a crack, and own a black cat. Forty percent own up to being a tad superstitious—occasionally crossing their fingers, for example.

One percent knocks on wood and avoids ladders, black cats, and anything to do with 13.

EVER HAD AN OUT-OF-BODY EXPERIENCE?

Roughly one in 10 guys claims to have seen a ghost, and one in five has sensed a strange presence in the room with him. More than half have experienced déjà vu (57 percent) and 64 percent believe in the devil. Almost half (49 percent) believe in ESP. Seven percent insist they've seen UFOs.

GET HIGH FROM NATURE?

Twenty-two percent of men say nature gives them a spiritual high, double the percentage of women who sense a larger design in the great outdoors.

HOW DO YOU FEEL ABOUT ASTROLOGY?

One in four American men believes in it, a number that keeps inching up. A third of 18- to 29-year-olds subscribe but only 18 percent of those 60 and older put any faith in it. Twelve percent checked their horoscope within the past day. Twenty-nine percent of men have gone to a fortune-teller to have their hands or Tarot cards read and six percent admit they've based a decision on their readings.

DO YOU BELIEVE THE SOUL SURVIVES AFTER DEATH?

Eighty-four percent of Americans do, but that includes 89 percent of women and only 78 percent of men. Twenty-three percent of guys believe they'll be reincarnated with five percent expecting to return as another life-form.

THINK JESUS WAS A REAL PERSON?

Three out of four people accept that Jesus actually lived and breathed. Another 16 percent mostly believe it while five percent chalk it up to a good story. More than one in every four men don't buy that Jesus was born to the Virgin Mary. Just over three out of every five men believe that Jesus will return to earth and more than a third think it will happen soon.

KNOW WHAT HAPPENED ON PALM SUNDAY AND GOOD FRIDAY?

Just one in three men knew that Jesus was supposed to have ridden into Jerusalem on a donkey with palm leaves laid in his path. But 52 percent knew that on Good Friday he was supposedly crucified.

DO YOU RELY ON PRAYER?

More than half of men (59 percent) pray often. Their prime reason is to seek guidance (62 percent), to give thanks or praise (54 percent), and to beg for forgiveness (47 percent). Forty-five percent ask specific favors from the deity such as to be healed. Amazingly, 14 percent of those without religion claim to pray every day. Forty-three percent of men incorporate prayer into their nighttime ritual. Yet only 26 percent find it the most gratifying spiritual activity they do. Nineteen percent of men say they've personally experienced the healing power of prayer.

FEEL YOU HAVE A PERSONAL GUARDIAN ANGEL?

Some 46 percent of guys believe they have been assigned an angel to assist them here on earth in various ways to make their life tick.

DO YOU APPROVE OF THE WORDS "IN GOD WE TRUST" ON COINS?

Nine out of ten men find nothing wrong with the inscription. And 78 percent find nothing wrong with nondenominational prayer at public school ceremonies. Seven out of ten wonder what the fuss is about over a Ten Commandments monument in a public building. But 64 percent disapprove of a monument of the Koran in a public school or government building.

DO YOU WANT TO BE ACTIVELY INVOLVED WITH A CHURCH?

Sixty-one percent of men (v. 69 percent of women) are members of a church. Thirty-five percent of men (v. 49 percent of women) say they strongly seek this connection. At the same time, 85 percent of American men consider themselves Christian (53 percent Protestant). Two percent are Jews and less than half of one percent, Muslims. More than two-thirds of women (69 percent), but just over half of men (53 percent), say religion is very important in their life.

DO YOU BELIEVE THAT WE'RE NOT ALONE?

Most men believe in aliens and are convinced they would be friendly if they ever visited earth. Three out of four people are sure life exists elsewhere in the universe. More than half feel the authorities have already covered up evidence of beings from other worlds. Forty-two percent of men and 38 percent of women think beings from other planets have visited earth.

DO YOU LET YOUR OUT-OF-THIS-WORLD FEELINGS INFLUENCE YOUR IN-THIS-WORLD ACTIONS?

Fifty-six percent of men acknowledge that their religious beliefs play some role in how they vote. Sixty-one percent think religion should influence public policy.

16

At the Gym: Babying and Buffing Bodies

MORE INTERESTED IN PARING THE DOUGH YOU OWE OR THE FLAB ON YOUR ABS?

More men are focused on fiscal fitness—shedding excess debt—than on physical fitness—losing weight (37 to 29 percent). One in four is equally focused on both.

SATISFIED WITH THE WAY YOU LOOK?

Men are more so than women, but there's plenty of room for dissatisfaction. Forty-three are down on their looks overall. Sixty-three percent are unhappy with their abdomens and 52 percent with their weight. (Twenty-two percent of those want to put on some pounds.) Forty-five percent wish they had better muscle tone and 38 percent a buffer chest.

AIMING FOR MUSCLE MASS?

Women prefer medium-built men with moderate biceps and pecs, but men are heavily into muscle mass and a competition body build. While only 27 percent think that men shown in bodybuilding magazines appeal to women (in fact, that turns on only one in five women) twice as many men as women say that bulging muscles matter to them.

REGULARLY MEASURE YOURSELF?

Gym rats do but not other guys. However, almost nine out of 10 men have measured their genitalia and most men admit they have been concerned about the size and shape of their parts.

HOW MUCH OF YOUR WEIGHT IS BODY FAT?

That depends on your age. The average 20-something guy has 17 percent of body fat. A decade later it's up to 20 percent. In his 40s the average guy's weight is 22 percent body fat; in his 50s it's up to 23 percent and 24 percent in his 60s.

IS YOUR BODY A TEMPLE OF ART?

Tattoos and body piercing decorate 16 percent of American men. Most of those who get a tattoo or body piercing do it because it makes them feel sexier or more rebellious. Seventeen percent who've gotten tattooed regret it—principally because they're no longer gung ho about the person named in the tattoo.

WHERE DO YOU EXERCISE?

Forty-three percent of men (v. 68 percent of women) do it at home. Twenty-six percent go outside. Nineteen percent sweat it off at the gym and 12 percent at work. Five percent avail themselves of community facilities and another five percent pump iron at an athletic or sports club.

HOW OFTEN?

Twenty-seven percent of men exercise daily—nine times as many as who sheepishly admit they never get around to it. Three out of five claim to exercise several times a week while eight percent are essentially weekend warriors. Still fewer than one in five exercises long enough to reap any health benefits and half bail out within six months of starting an exercise program.

WHATCHA DOING AT THE GYM?

Not aerobics. While this is hot with one in 10 women only three percent of guys do aerobics. Fourteen percent go in for weight lifting, 14 percent jog, and five percent often ride a stationary bike. The top exercise activity for both men and women is walking.

WHAT BOTHERS YOU MOST AT THE GYM?

Annoying people who steal the equipment you've waited for or the jerk who barks into his cell phone while hogging a bike are the biggest peeves. Lesser ones marked for banishment include guys who sit on a machine while they rest between sets, or cover the timer with a towel, or leave lots of extra weight plates on a bar and "forget" to return the weights to their designated spot on the rack. The most common reason guys give for not going to the gym is that it's too crowded, that they don't know what they're doing, and that they'll be the only one there who isn't buff.

WORK OUT WITH A PERSONAL TRAINER?

Eighteen percent of men have worked out with a personal trainer. The likeliest to seek one-on-one training are 18-to 24-year-olds (28 percent) and those making at least $65,000 per year (29 percent).

ARE YOU A GYM THUG?

Only one in six men admits he congregates around a piece of equipment—usually the bench press—like a hungry lion around a zebra carcass.

BELIEVE THAT WITHOUT PAIN THERE'S NO GAIN?

More than half of guys think they've got to work at top intensity in order to benefit, despite the fact that moderate-intensity exercise lowers the risk of dying just as much as high-intensity exercise and can highlight those pecs just as well also.

GONE TO AN EXERCISE CLASS?

Twelve percent of men have, compared to 22 percent of women. Seventy-two percent claim to break a sweat; 37 percent walk away drenched. Nearly 2 million hard-core fitness buffs and those sorely lacking in coordination are in group cycling classes.

PREFER AN ALL-MALE PLACE TO SWEAT?

Forty-three percent of men do, if given the choice, possibly because it lessens the intimidation of not knowing how to use the equipment. That doesn't mean they don't like to watch girls work out. Fifty-three percent consider watching gym babes' hard bodies on the machines the best spectator sport they enjoy.

OWN WEIGHTS?

Half of men (49 percent) claim to. Twelve percent also own an exercise leotard. Some 51.6 million individuals in the U.S. trained with some form of free weights in a recent year and 30 million of them used weight resistance machines.

HOW MUCH ARE YOU PUMPING?

Researchers suggest men lift at least 60 percent of the maximum weight they can to boost the size of their muscles, but very, very few stack enough weight plates on the pile to change the shape of their muscles. Few novice weight lifters understand that maxing out—slowly increasing the amount of iron they pump until they're lifting to fatigue (that is, to the most they possibly can)—is the way to get the most benefit from a workout.

WHAT DO YOU SAY TO
SOMEONE WHO HOGS THE TREADMILL?

You could say, "You've been on the thing for the past half hour and while I'm impressed with your stamina, the sign over there says there's a 20-minute limit during peak periods. If I could use the treadmill in the next five minutes, I'd be grateful." But most likely you'd tell her that no matter how hard she cranks it, it won't do her a bit of good and she'll still be a dried-up old date-less fig.

HOW MANY PUSH-UPS CAN YOU DO?

A buff 26 percent of men boast they can do more than 40 in one sitting and another 17 percent preen that they can do between 30 and 40. Twenty-six percent confess they couldn't complete even 10.

HOW ABOUT CHIN-UPS?

Assuming it's from a stationary straight arm hang to chin above the bar, 35 percent of guys say they can do 10 or more and another 15 percent weigh in at six to nine. Seventeen percent say they can accomplish three to five and 13 percent figure they can do one or two. Six percent beg not to have to try.

CAN YOU LIFT HALF YOUR BODY WEIGHT ABOVE YOUR HEAD?

Almost three out of five guys (58 percent) say they can but another 19 percent haven't a clue as they've never tried to. Only 10 percent have attempted this and gone down in defeat.

SWIM 400 METERS WITHOUT A BREAK?

Six percent of men would never try: they can't swim. Another 14 percent would be what camps call minnows. Twenty-eight percent consider themselves very strong swimmers and another 26 percent figure they could probably swim that far uninterrupted.

USUALLY STRETCH BEFORE EXERCISE?

Fewer than one in three men limber their muscles before putting them through their paces.

CAN YOU TOUCH YOUR TOES?

The average guy in his 20s can sit and reach 17.5 inches (or 2.5 inches beyond his toes). That shrinks to 16.5 inches (or 1.5 inches beyond his toes) in his 30s, and 15.3 inches (or 0.3 inches beyond his toes) in his 40s. By the time he's in his 50s his reach has dwindled to 14.5 inches (within 0.5 inches of his toes) and by his 60s the average man can extend 13.5 inches (or within 1.5 inches of his toes).

HOW HIGH CAN YOU JUMP?

The average 20-something guy can jump 20.5 inches off the floor. That shrinks to 19.5 inches in his 30s, 16 inches in his 40s, and 14 inches in his 50s. Don't ask him to get off the ground after that.

HOW MANY SQUATS CAN YOU DO?

The average 18- to 25-year-old guy can squat 35 to 38 times in one session. The average aging gent (56 years old on up) can do 16 to 19. Thirty-six- to 45-year-old guys can do 27 to 29 squats on average.

WHAT BODY PART DO YOU WORK ON MOST?

The chest ranks as the number one body part to work on (40 percent) far eclipsing arm workouts (29 percent).

HOW MUCH CAN YOU BENCH PRESS?

Forty-one percent of guys can do just the bar and 51 percent, their own weight. Eight percent consider themselves powerful lifters.

DO YOU VARY YOUR ROUTINE?

While 13 percent who are fixated on their arms or chest, say, utilize the same piece of equipment in the same sequence virtually all the time, 87 percent of those at the gym mix it up.

TRIED PILATES?

Some 9.5 million Americans participated in this hybrid stretching/resistance activity—but 89 percent of them were female.

HOW ABOUT YOGA?

While yoga has 15 million adherents, 77 percent of them are women. Yogis (as male practitioners are called) tend to avoid the chanting and New Age vibes in favor of the more athletic, fast-moving styles such as Vinyasa and Ashtanga, otherwise known as power yoga.

DO ANY MARTIAL ARTS?

Five percent of adults in this country (9.4 million of them) have tried to reduce cinder blocks with their bare hands at least once in a recent year, and according to Simmons Market Research, 28 percent of them practice it often. Fifty-two percent of those "artists" are male and most are young. Fewer than five percent of American men have practiced any form of the ancient martial art Tai Chi.

USE THE TRENDIEST CARDIO MACHINE, THE ELLIPTICAL TRAINER?

The treadmill is American men's most popular cardio machine, but 27 percent prefer the elliptical.

DO YOU COVER UP IN A PUBLIC LOCKER ROOM?

At the gym, the "Y," the pool, or wherever guys take to the showers, seven out of ten let it all hang out. At the same time, fewer than one in five admits to flexing to show off his abs and pecs.

DO YOU ALWAYS WIPE UP AFTER YOURSELF?

Sure, no one wants to use equipment that's been marinated in your bodily fluids but that doesn't stop half of the guys from admitting that they don't always wipe off the equipment. Thirty-nine percent say they usually do and 32 percent wonder why they should.

GUILTY OF LOUD MOANING AND GRUNTING?

While it may signal that you're really serious about your training and working real hard to meet goals, it also announces to the rest of the world that you're an attention-seeking moron. Still, one in ten guys admits he may sound like a one-man maternity ward. (On the other hand, according to Durex, one in 20 men cums while working out.)

INTO KICKBALL?

Tired of competitive office sports teams that offer too little camaraderie, lots of grown-up guys are flocking to kickball for the fun. The World Kickball Association has almost 10,000 members in the D.C. area alone.

HOW ABOUT BOXING?

Some places call it box-aerobics. Others label it cardiobox. Some refer to it as slug-mania. Whatever you call it boxing is becoming a heavyweight at gyms. Twenty-one percent of all U.S. health clubs now offer boxing classes, or some offshoot of them, according to the American Council on Exercise. And that figure is rising.

JUMP ROPE?

While rope jumping fries 600 to 1,000 calories an hour (at 120 jumps a minute) and improves cardiovascular fitness, balance, and agility, fewer than one in 10 men in the gym regularly do it.

Say—Can You Do That?

- One in four guys can cross his eyes and one in three can flare his nostrils.
- Men are almost four times as likely as women to be able to whistle loudly to hail cabs or other people. Twenty-three percent say it's part of their daily vocabulary.
- Almost one in four of all men can juggle; only one in 10 women can.
- Almost 21 of every 100 women in America are double-jointed but only 14 percent of men are. Fewer than one in ten men can do a split.
- 21 percent can blow smoke rings and 24 percent can spit bubbles.
- 30 percent of men can raise one eyebrow at a time.
- Two out of three can snap their fingers.
- Just 13 percent of men can wiggle their ears.
- One in four can cross his eyes.
- Roughly two in three can roll their tongues into a coiled U-position; only five percent can reach the tips of their nose with their tongues.

Are You "Guilty"?

- 46 percent of men often jiggle their knees when sitting.
- 10 percent are left-handed (only 8 percent of women are).
- 16 percent stutter.
- 40 percent crack their knuckles.
- 27 percent regularly chew on a pen or pencil.
- 38 percent peel the labels off bottles or cans.
- 10 to 20 percent grind their teeth.
- 8 percent are color-blind.
- 18 percent sometimes bite their fingernails.

➤ 50 plus percent usually pick off their scabs. Oddly, left-handers are likelier to do so than right-handed guys.

➤ 68 percent jingle the coins in their pockets.

17

Holidays and Vacations

CONSIDER SUPER BOWL SUNDAY A HOLIDAY?

Men recognize it as a high holy day of commercialism but it's an even bigger at-home party occasion than New Year's Eve. (On average, each Super Bowl party hosts 17 people.) The only day they eat more is on Thanksgiving. And the only days they drink more alcohol are New Year's and St. Patrick's Day. One in four guys participates in an office betting pool and six percent of workers usually call in sick on the Monday after. Seagram's found 53 percent of guys would prefer two tickets to the game over a night on the town with a gorgeous woman. At the game, 28 percent would wear a team jersey, 16 percent would swap old stories with their buddies, and 16 percent would overeat.

DOES VALENTINE'S DAY MOVE YOU?

Seventy-six percent of men say the holiday is too commercial and 68 percent say there's too much pressure to celebrate it, but 77 percent (willingly or grudgingly) indulge in this love fest. Two-thirds consider themselves romantics. Thirty-two percent send flowers. (Most of those selected are roses, with red being the preferred shade.) Men are three times more likely to give jewelry than women are. They're more interested in receiving chocolates than anything else. While women are often thought to be the more romantic gender, Valentine's Day seems to be more important to men.

WHAT COMES TO MIND ABOUT EASTER?

Some 44 percent of men say the religious aspect is not too significant to them, but they're five times likelier to think of Jesus on the cross as they are to muse about Easter eggs or jelly beans. Nearly half of men (48 percent) personally believe that Jesus rose from the dead. A third usually go to a church service at some point over the weekend. As for their favorite Easter candy, 36 percent want chocolate bunnies and for one in four, marshmallow peeps. One in five loves the chocolate eggs and 18 percent, jelly beans.

HONOR MOM ON HER DAY?

The National Retail Federation says 87 percent of sons celebrate Mother's Day and spend an average of $113.98 on the old lady (vs. $81.69 shelled out by daughters). Most buy traditional gifts like jewelry, facials or massages, clothes, gift certificates, housewares, and flowers. More people celebrate dinner out on Mother's Day than on any other occasion other than birthdays—and they, of course, are spread out over the year.

AND DAD ON HIS?

It may be another manufactured holiday but 83 percent of sons celebrate it. Sixty-five percent send a card. Those doing more than a call or visit spend an average $52.30 for dad. (Daughters traditionally spend more here than sons.) One in five dads will get something to wear while 15 percent will get some home improvement or gardening tool or appliance. Fourteen percent will receive a gift certificate.

WHAT'S YOUR FAVORITE SUMMER HOLIDAY?

It wasn't just the movie that made *Independence* Day a hit: even before that 64 percent of Americans thought this event defined summer. For 22 percent the high point of this season is Memorial Day while 13 percent most enjoy Labor Day. One percent consider Flag Day their favorite summer holiday.

SO HOW DO YOU CELEBRATE?

Fireworks, of course. Even if they're not the actual pyromaniac, 82 percent of men will ooh and aah at them (including the 13 percent who watch it on mosquito-free TV). Twenty-nine percent usually watch a parade (five percent even march in one).

TRICK OR TREAT?

Seven out of ten men dispense treats on Halloween—mostly packaged sweets such as Snickers and stashes of pennies, according to Market Facts. Another 26 percent turn out the lights and pretend not to be at home. Thirteen percent don a holiday costume, seven percent visit a haunted house, nearly one in three attends or gives a party, and six percent watch a scary movie. Fourteen percent decorate their home. Twelve percent object on religious grounds to celebrating Halloween.

WHERE DO YOU CELEBRATE THANKSGIVING?

Eleven percent of Americans celebrate Thanksgiving at a restaurant with men more likely than women to do so. Baby boomers and those even older are most likely to host at home. The average Thanksgiving feast has five to 10 people digging in together.

IF YOU COOK AT HOME
THIS DAY, GET ANY COMMERCIAL HELP?

If by commercial help you mean a precooked turkey, forget it. According to National Restaurant Association research, only 34 percent of Americans would rely on food prepared away from home for part of their Thanksgiving meal. Generally, younger adults are more likely to use food items prepared at a restaurant as part of what goes on their Thanksgiving table.

WHAT'S FOR DINNER?

There's a reason they call it turkey day, yet 23 percent of families serve ham, chicken, or Italian dishes. For one in five the stuffing is a favorite side dish. As for pie, this is pumpkin's starring moment: half as many prefer chocolate cream or apple or pecan pie. On the seamy side of this sunny holiday, 26 percent of feasters say they're still dining on Thanksgiving s'mores six days later.

HANG A XMAS STOCKING?

If you're a dad you do—as well as leave out cookies and milk or some other treat for Santa and pay the dude a visit. Nineteen percent go out Christmas caroling. Another 42 percent plan to meet their sweetie under a sprig of mistletoe during the holiday season. Almost three out of four attend a religious service over the holiday.

AND THE TREE?

Fifty-four percent of households put up some sort of Christmas tree. Maybe because the needles shed, fake trees outnumber real ones.

WHEN DO YOU START
LISTENING TO CHRISTMAS MUSIC?

Eleven percent never do. They find the tunes depressing. But even more (14 percent) keep that festival sound going year round. Thirty-two percent save it for the week or so before Christmas while another 30 percent start when holiday shopping season erupts, right after Thanksgiving.

DRINK EGGNOG; ROAST CHESTNUTS?

Despite its waist-expanding properties, 53 percent of men usually drink eggnog during the holiday season. But despite Nat King Cole's famous song, only nine percent roast chestnuts on an open fire or otherwise.

WHAT'S FOR CHRISTMAS DINNER?

Thanksgiving isn't the only turkey derby. The big bird is on 37 percent of Christmas tabletops while 23 percent of Noel revelers eat ham, according to NPD. Another 25 percent forswear the fancy foods and chow down on a sandwich. Eleven percent of diners eat pasta and 10 percent, a beef dish—most likely roast beef.

STEPPING OUT?

The average guy will go to 2.7 parties this holiday season and spend two hours and 36 minutes at each. (Fourteen percent are attracted by the free food and booze.) Chances are he'll bring a gift. Instead of frankincense, gold, and myrrh it's probably cookies, candy, or booze. Three percent often regift, that is, pass on a present given to them.

PAY IN POUNDS?

Just 44 percent of men expect they won't gain any weight during the holidays. Nineteen percent anticipate adding a pound or two and 26 percent figure they'll gain three to five pounds. Five percent expect to pack on an additional six to 10 pounds. An unfortunate one percent expect to add even more.

GOT GIFTS?

More men start Christmas shopping earlier than women (six months ahead of time, anyone?), but more than twice as many men as women begin in late December. A third of men say they have trouble buying gifts for their spouse while just seven percent admit they have trouble buying gifts for children. Forty-four percent have avoided shopping altogether by just giving cash. Three out of four families who exchange gifts at the Christmas holiday open them on Christmas Day; one in four can't wait and tears into them on Christmas Eve.

WHAT DO YOU DO WITH MISFIT GIFTS?

Few men go through the trouble of returning unwanted gifts. A third shove them to the back of the closet; slightly fewer use them anyway, and another third give them away, either as a "regift" or as used goods. While three out of five guys don't feel hurt if their sweetie exchanges their gift, 35 percent admit to feeling stung. Another five percent say they're too busy returning their own gifts to care.

KEEP THE CARDS?

Fifty-two percent of men usually hold on to the Christmas cards they receive. Just 26 percent usually throw them all away at holiday's end.

WHEN DO YOU TAKE DOWN THE DECORATIONS?

While 14 percent clean up the day after Christmas, 62 percent go into fifth gear the day after New Year's. Sixteen percent don't face that problem: they never got around to putting them up.

WHAT ARE YOU DOING NEW YEAR'S EVE?

Forget the noisemakers, top hats, and champagne, many of you will be staying home. In a recent year, 28 percent of guys claimed they did nothing special at all. Almost half watched TV, while 10 percent rented a movie for the DVD. Twenty-three percent even went to bed before midnight. Just one in five expects to party past the ball drop; two percent even expect to put on formal duds.

MAKE A RESOLUTION?

Alas, that seems to be going out of style. Despite a devotion to self-improvement, only 35 percent of men (and 39 percent of women) made a New Year's resolution in 2004. The most popular decision is to exercise more followed by to spend more time with family, to pay off debt, and to diet. Fifty-five percent of those who've made a New Year's resolution failed to follow through, largely because of lack of willpower.

And Vacations

DO YOU LIVE FOR VACATION?

While 31 percent say that's their number, 21 percent love to work so much that vacation isn't on their wish lists. Forty-three percent consider every day in life a vacation—so no need to change routine.

TAKE ONE IN THE PAST YEAR?

Eighty-six percent of guys 18 to 49 have vacationed at least once in the past year. One in five has taken at least five trips. Sightseeing and relaxing are their top two experiences. Partying is important to one-third of guys, especially younger ones. One in four is interested in meeting people and hooking up.

WHERE ARE YOU HEADED?

If it's a domestic trip, the destination could well be Florida, Las Vegas, California, or Hawaii. Florida tops the list. Seventy percent of men have visited Disneyland or Disney World. If the guy has a female partner, more often than not she picks the place. If he's a dad, in more than one in three situations the kids have a big say in deciding the destination.

WHAT'S THE BIGGEST BOTHER ON A FLIGHT?

It's pretty much neck and neck—or lap and butt—with the guy in front reclining his seat to the max and the kid in back kicking your seat. Only 23 percent of men claim to get bothered by a seatmate who spreads into their personal space (this grates many more women), and only seven percent are ticked off by chatty fellow passengers. Even fewer are irked by being wedged in their seat (dis)courtesy of a sleeping seatmate. Needing to use the loo, half of men say they'd wake the fellow passenger while 41 percent would try to gingerly climb over him without disturbing him. Just four percent are annoyed by the lack of space in the overhead.

HOW ABOUT ON THE TRIP OVERALL?

Flight delays are more aggravating than lack of legroom and poor in-flight service. On arrival at the destination lost hotel bookings was a major source of annoyance. Flight restrictions on tickets caused problems for many travelers. Inflated hotel telephone charges round out the most annoying problems for travelers.

EVER GET MOTION SICKNESS?

Sure it's likelier to affect children riding in a car or adults braving rough seas in small watercraft but at one time or another half of all guys experienced motion sickness including many who never went to sea.

WHAT'S YOUR FAVORITE TIME FOR A GETAWAY?

While 32 percent pick summer for their "perfect vacation," 27 percent opt to take time off in the fall; 21 percent, in the spring; and 19 percent, in winter.

EXPECT TO ATTEND A FAMILY REUNION?

Some 62 percent of men will go to a family reunion this year, predicts Bruskin Research. Whether or not they do depends a lot on how far they live from their family's central axis. Only 56 percent of those who live at least 300 miles from their family show up at the jamboree.

HOW DO YOU SPEND YOUR CAREFREE VACATION HOURS?

Certainly not just vegging out on a beach. Men prefer activities or sightseeing to lazing and relaxing by a two-to-one margin. Cultural activities attract nearly twice as many guys as getting a suntan does.

WOULD YOU CHANGE TRAVEL PLANS IF A PSYCHIC ADVISED IT?

One-third (36 percent) of men say they would reorganize their trip if the stars suggested they should. Fifty-six percent would discount the advice and stay the course.

DO YOU USUALLY BUY TRIP INSURANCE?

Two out of three vacationers—68 percent—plunk down when going someplace exotic.

NOSH ON THE MINIBAR?

Around 30 percent of travelers won't dare touch the minibar where five dollars for a bag of nuts is the norm.

PLAN YOUR VACATION WHILE AT WORK?

Only 18 percent of men (v. 11 percent of women) steal time on the job to plan their vacation, either because they're too busy at work or because they fear they're being monitored. Big wage earners are the most likely to make their travel plans at work.

WORRIED ABOUT TERRORISM?

Even if they're not headed to the Middle East, 14 percent of men admit they're a tad queasy about terrorism when they travel.

WHERE DO YOU USUALLY
GO WRONG REGARDING VACATION?

Forty-three percent say their biggest mistake is not taking off enough time. Seventeen percent berate themselves for not being able to relax or get their mind off work. Eight percent castigate themselves for checking in with the office often, and seven percent scold themselves for not preparing or organizing their work well prior to leaving.

GET TESTY WITH YOUR PARTNER ON VACATION?

Fifty-four percent of men who've traveled with a S.O. find themselves in a snit on vacation. Fifty-six percent of arguers argue about how much money to spend, 45 percent go at each other over what activities to do, and 35 percent get sore deciding where to go at all.

EVER TAKE A VACATION AT HOME?

Not counting a second or vacation home, within the last year 18.5 percent of men have stayed home during vacation time they've taken from work.

GOT A PASSPORT?

Only 27 percent of American men currently hold a valid passport and just 42 percent have ever had one. One in four has never left these shores, and just 36 percent have visited more than two countries. Still, men tend to be more widely traveled than women. For those who have ventured beyond our borders, men have visited an average of 4.4 countries compared to 2.9 for women. Canada and Mexico are the top two international destinations visited, followed by continental Europe, the Caribbean, and England.

FOLLOW AIRLINES' ENTREATIES
TO TURN OFF YOUR CELL PHONE?

In the dark ages, before discussion of allowing cell phone usage in the skies, everyone complied with the captain's request to turn off the phones. Upon landing, though, men are more likely than women to not wait until they're inside the terminal to reconnect, according to Fodor's. Twenty-four percent of them grab their phone as soon as the plane hits the runway—more than twice as many as women.

UNPACK OR ADJUST THE TEMPERATURE?

Nearly 31 percent of guys first head to the thermostat control when they check into a hotel room, surpassing the 29 percent who start to unpack and hang up clothes and the 19 percent who flip on the TV. Ten percent say they first check out the safety instructions on the back of the door and six percent look in the minibar or get ice for the room.

OFTEN GO BACK FOR FORGOTTEN
ITEMS BEFORE OFFICIALLY STARTING OUT?

False starts, it seems, are as American as apple pie. Almost three out of four travelers go back to check that the stove is off or grab their hotel reservations left on the table, according to Avis Rent A Car.

TAKE ANYTHING NOT
NAILED DOWN AT THE HOTEL?

Lots of travelers take home "souvenirs." What most often "mistakenly" make their way into men's luggage are towels, ashtrays, bathrobes, and bath mats. More than three out of five snag the toiletries left in the bathroom—the same percent of pet owners who have snuck their pooch or tabby into the room. One in three men ages 18 to 34 admits to raiding the housekeeper's cart in the hallway when the attendant isn't looking.

OFTEN LEAVE THE ROOM A MESS?

Twenty-five percent of hotel guests leave wet towels on the floor. Nine percent eat in bed leaving crumbly messes, and 13 percent leave the television on when they check out.

USE THE WAKE-UP SERVICE?

One in three hotel guests brings his own alarm clock because he doesn't trust the hotel to wake him up. The most common wake-up time in hotels is 7:00 A.M.

WHAT'S MOST IMPORTANT IN PICKING A HOTEL?

For women, it's service. For men, location, according to Wyndham Hotels. While women also appreciate a deep tub—not just a shower stall—just 14 percent of the men soaked their cares away in tubs.

DO YOU FEEL MORE STRESS
DAYS AFTER YOU RETURN TO WORK?

The relaxing benefits of a holiday don't last long. Israeli researchers from Tel Aviv University found stress levels drop during a two-week holiday but start to rise again within three days after people return to work. And three weeks after a holiday, workers were just as stressed as they were before.

DO YOU TAKE SHORT BREAKS—SUCH AS
WEEKENDS AWAY—OR SAVE FOR BIG LONG ONES?

How about not take any at all? That's the situation for 12 percent of American workers, according to Expedia.com. Many more take only a part of what's "owed" them. The leading reason: too much to do. Nearly a quarter of vacationers said time off made them feel guilty. Vacations average 14 days—the fewest of any first world country.

USUALLY BINGE EAT ON VACATION?

Almost two out of three men—64 percent—often overeat while traveling. And 59 percent admit chowing on something unhealthy that they wouldn't touch at home. For more than half—55 percent—holiday travel is the most dangerous for their waistline and circadian rhythm: 41 percent say holiday travel disrupts everything from sleep to keeping fit and 20 percent find it even more stressful than a business trip, going to the dentist, even getting married!

DO YOU REGULARLY CHECK
FOR YOUR TRAVEL DOCUMENTS?

A fourth of men check repeatedly to make sure they still have their airline ticket. And while 55 percent claim they don't check often, they admit they have set strategies to keep themselves constantly aware of where their documents are. Just a fifth casually put the ticket in their bag or pocket and don't think about it until it's needed.

WHAT'S THE LEAST YOU ACCEPT TO BE
BUMPED TO A LATER FLIGHT?

While three percent would eschew any offer, 55 percent would drive a very hard bargain: a round-trip ticket anywhere in the country. Seventeen percent would be content with an upgrade to first class on the next flight. Twelve percent would vacate their seat for $400.

HOW MUCH WOULD YOU
SHELL OUT FOR A FLIGHT IN SPACE?

Not a penny, say half of guys who have zero interest. One in five would clamber into a space suit if it was for free. Two percent would pay over $50,000 for the experience.

ROAD WARRIORS: WHAT
GIZMOS DO YOU TAKE ON THE ROAD?

More than three out of four frequent business travelers bring a cell phone, according to Greenfield Online, and 53 percent tote a laptop. A third take a pager, and 12 percent use a personal digital assistant.

WHEN TRAVELING FOR BUSINESS, WHICH ITEM DO YOU FORGET MOST OFTEN?

Some 31 percent have forgotten a cell phone charger, 21 percent have left behind a razor, and 19 percent have hit the road sans toothpaste.

HOW DO YOU SPEND TIME ON A BUSINESS FLIGHT?

Even though the trip is designated for business purposes, most men will read, sleep, or watch the movie in that order, before pulling out the work.

BOTHERED BY BEING A ROAD WARRIOR?

Seventy-three percent of road warriors fret about the work not being done back at the office while an equal number worry about being away from home and family. But the gender split here is a chasm—84 percent of women and 69 percent of men. Fifty-nine percent of women v. 42 percent of men fret a lot about errands, bills, pets, the whole empire they've left untended while on the road. One in four finds business travel the least favorite part of his job.

WOULD YOU PUT ON THE BRAKES IF YOU COULD?

A third of business travelers would surrender their frequent flier miles and the duties that go with them right away if it would not

handcuff their careers. Fifty-two percent would reject a job offer if it required too much travel.

HOW LONG DOES IT TAKE YOU TO RECOVER?

Assuming it's a coast-to-coast flight or farther, more than half
of business travelers need at least a day to physically recover
from their trip. Hyatt Hotels figures it takes the average worker
2.4 days to catch up at work and 2.2 days to catch up at home.

WOULD YOU SKIP A CHILD'S BIRTHDAY PARTY TO ATTEND AN IMPORTANT CLIENT MEETING?

Forty-five percent of executives would go if called. They'd pass
on Christmas with the family, a funeral, even a relative's wedding to see He-Who-Pays-the-Bills when bidden. Four in five
dads with young children admit they would travel on their wee
ones' birthdays. Women warriors are less likely to willingly miss
a child's birthday or Christmas. Thirty-eight percent of men
have missed their own wedding anniversaries because of business travel.

GET LONELY ON THE ROAD?

Almost half of business travelers (47 percent) feel lonesome and
nine percent find it acutely depressing. For 12 percent, business
travel activates their juices. It seems salespeople deserve their
reputation as Romeos of the road: one in three flirts with
strangers on business trips. Two percent of business travelers
have met their future spouse on a business trip.

EVER HAD TO BUY CLOTHES IN AN EMERGENCY ON A BUSINESS TRIP?

Almost two out of three business travelers have had to do some emergency shopping. The most frequently purchased items to replace those left behind are shirts followed by ties and then socks and belts. Eight percent have had to replace everything because of lost luggage.

HOW ABOUT SURRENDER YOUR AIR MILES?

Forty-three percent of employees complain they're forced to pony up their air miles to the company rather than enjoy them personally.

18

At Leisure:
Men . . . o . . . pause

YAWN: HOW OFTEN ARE YOU BORED SILLY?

American men may have tuned out demands from their partner, but few have tuned out altogether. Sixty-three percent of guys say they're rarely bored and another 16 percent claim they never are. What do they do when they are in this state? Rather than stare into space, apathetic and listless, most turn on the boob tube—or switch channels. But 44 percent say that when they're in a rut, they often head to the fridge. While most men don't associate any particular time of the week with boredom, 13 percent pick any time on Sunday as the most likely prospect as the least interesting part of the week.

Boob Tube

DO YOU FALL ASLEEP WITH THE TV OR RADIO ON?

For more than one of every five men, what's on is better than a sleeping pill. Twenty-two percent almost always fall asleep clutching the remote control (or having it slither from their relaxed hand) while 55 percent do sometimes. Southerners and Northeasterners are far more likely than Westerners to do so. Just 15 percent of men say they're always attentive watchers and listeners.

WHAT TURNS YOU ON . . . OR WHAT DO YOU TURN ON?

Men watch more movies than anything else with sports a close second. As for serials, police/detective shows are more popular than sitcoms, which are more popular than documentaries. Home improvement shows edge out reality TV and game shows slightly nudge past talk shows, according to BIGresearch. Men watch more cooking shows than cartoons.

WHICH CABLE NETWORK DO YOU WATCH REGULARLY?

That depends big time on your age. Almost 40 percent of men 35 and older watch a lot of the Discovery Channel, 35 percent the History Channel, and 33 percent A&E, Sci Fi, and ESPN. For younger guys the Discovery Channel gets real competition from Comedy Central. Younger guys are also very likely to be watching TNT, Spike TV, Sci Fi, and ESPN.

RATHER WATCH *SURVIVOR* OR PLAY DOOM?

Eight of 10 men 18 to 34 years old would rather give up their game console for a month than forsake TV. But the game industry's Entertainment Software Association notes that more than half of them are watching less TV now, and spending more time on video and computer games. Forty-one percent of men find the Internet more interesting than TV. Just 26 percent are uninterested in the Web.

WHEN WATCHING TV, DO YOU MULTITASK?

When they watch prime-time TV twice as many men as women do nothing else (12 v. 5 percent). Four out of 10 men routinely flip between channels, almost twice the number of female channel surfers. Many more women than men often watch TV "by appointment."

ANY IDEA HOW LONG YOU SPEND SEARCHING FOR THE REMOTE?

You may not know it but IKEA studied this and found the average Joe spends 80 minutes a week searching for the remote. Women spend a mere seven minutes a week.

GET INTO FANTASY FOOTBALL CONTESTS?

For the four months of fall and through the NFL play-offs and Super Bowl, 14 million men pore over statistics, make roster adjustments, and initiate player trades in thousands of fantasy football contests.

WHAT DO YOU DO WHEN YOU'RE HOME ALONE ON A FRIDAY NIGHT?

Finding themselves at a loose end, two-thirds of men are likely to turn on the tube. While women are more likely to go to bed early and read, men are likely to catch up on work and break out the snacks. Thirteen percent boot up for pleasure and five percent do chores.

UNWIND WITH A BEER?

It's no wonder there are so many beer bellies: 37 million men regularly knock one back. The biggest guzzlers live in Nevada while men from Utah imbibe the least. Fifty-eight percent of men stopped in a bar or tavern in the past year and 40 percent regard a drink or two at the end of the day as a perfect antidote to a stressful day. Just eight percent of guys have one regular bar where they hang out.

HOW OFTEN DO YOU TAKE DAYTIME NAPS?

Twelve percent of men never take a siesta and another 31 percent rarely do. Just 14 percent indulge in this pleasure daily.

GOT SOME SORT OF SECRET HANDSHAKE OR PASSWORD GOING?

Fifty-four percent of men belong to at least one members-only club—a fraternity, veterans' club, fraternal order, country or civic club, church, union . . . even the PTA counts. Women are likelier to join groups: 58 percent of them belong to at least one club, like an art association or religious group.

GO OUT OR STAY IN?

While 61 percent of men (and 69 percent of women) enjoy parties, 78 percent say they'd rather spend a quiet evening at home than go out to one.

Fanzine

WHAT'S YOUR FAVORITE SPECTATOR SPORT?

Professional football leads baseball by a two to one margin as guys' favorite sport. But NASCAR is fast zooming into second place as fewer guys describe themselves as diehard baseball fans. Guys are also gluttons for college basketball.

AND LEAST FAVORITE?

Dog fighting and pro wrestling with steroid-pumped madmen slamming each other around the ring are the most detested "sports" in America, according to the Sports Marketing Group in Atlanta. Guys also dislike bullfighting and pro boxing. Many resent the arrogant, undisciplined behavior of the pro athletes and their inordinate salaries.

- ➤ 74 percent follow professional football. Their top five teams are the Dallas Cowboys, Green Bay Packers, Oakland Raiders, Tampa Bay Buccaneers, and San Francisco 49ers.
- ➤ 31 percent describe themselves as ice hockey fans. Twenty-two percent have gone to a game in the past two years and nine percent even bought some team merchandise.
- ➤ 4 percent have bet on a horse race in the past year.
- ➤ 34 percent follow college football avidly. Their favorite teams are Notre Dame, Florida State, Penn State, Ohio State, and Oklahoma.
- ➤ 20 percent follow men's college basketball and seven percent watch women's basketball.
- ➤ 39 percent describe themselves as rabid NASCAR fans. Three percent are super-fans of Formula 1 racing.
- ➤ 33 percent like to watch figure skating (v. 58 percent of women).

- ➤ 44 percent watch professional baseball games although 73 percent would favor a players' salary cap.
- ➤ 4 percent have placed a bet on the NCAA basketball tournament in a pool with friends or coworkers.
- ➤ 43 percent are basketball fans.
- ➤ 15 percent have bet on a professional sports event in the past 12 months.

Hobby Horse

- ➤ 33 percent worked on a collection such as stamps, coins, or rocks.
- ➤ 39 percent worked on a crafts project such as model building. There are 18 million nonprofessional woodworkers in America, 90 percent of whom are male.
- ➤ 4 percent draw, paint, or sculpt.
- ➤ 20 percent do some form of creative writing.
- ➤ 27 percent play an instrument or sing.
- ➤ 3 percent dabble in photography—though few of the shots on their digital cameras have ever left their hard drives.
- ➤ 6 percent have acted in a play at some time in their lives or dabbled in some form of filmmaking.
- ➤ 2.6 percent are into antiques.
- ➤ 19 percent like to dance.
- ➤ 13 percent have gone to a topless bar or strip club (v. four percent of women).
- ➤ 66 percent like to go to the beach.
- ➤ 16 percent have visited an aquarium in the last 12 months: 28 percent, the zoo; and 35 percent, a historic place or toured buildings or neighborhoods.
- ➤ 60 percent went on a picnic in the past year.

How Active were You . . . in the Past Year?

- ➤ 24 percent of men went camping.
- ➤ 31 percent went hiking, including 18 percent who backpacked at least once a year.
- ➤ 6.2 percent went canoeing.
- ➤ 17 percent have thrown darts.
- ➤ 4.5 percent have dabbled in archery.
- ➤ 9.3 percent have gone horseback riding in the past five years and six percent have done so more than once.
- ➤ 5 percent played badminton.
- ➤ 1 percent have gone bird-watching.
- ➤ 26 percent have gone motor or power boating.
- ➤ 24 percent play golf. If they could tee off at any course in the world, more would choose Pebble Beach than anywhere else, followed by Augusta National and then St. Andrews.
- ➤ 23 percent have played board games.
- ➤ 38 percent have recently ridden a bicycle for pleasure (and 19 percent claim to do so often).
- ➤ 36 percent went fishing.
- ➤ 41 percent have gone sailing.
- ➤ Just under seven percent have gone ice skating.
- ➤ 3.3 percent went mountain or rock climbing.
- ➤ 16 percent hunted in the past year.
- ➤ 24 percent have played billiards.

ARE YOU A POOL SHARK?

One in five don't even know which end of the stick to pick up. Just seven percent boast they can run the table with ease. Three out of four play but know they can get sharked.

A TAILGATER?

Marketers are calling it the new American community: more than 30 million Americans have tailgated in the past year and 71 percent of them have done so at least six times (usually aiming for the same spot in the parking lot). Amazingly, 30 percent of football tailgaters don't actually attend the game.

A COASTER KING?

Almost one in four men (24 percent) have rolled and twisted through more than 1.5 billion scream machines and attractions at America's 450 fixed-site amusement parks in the last 12 months. Forty percent of the time, they shelled out more money here than they'd expected to. While they liked the experience overall, 24 percent were discouraged by the crowds and long lines and the theme-park food.

A CINEPHILE?

Almost three in every four men (74 percent) went to the movies at least once last year. Young men are the biggest audience. Eighty-nine percent of moviegoers head to the concession stand. If they've arrived at the theater late, 43 percent buy a ticket and go in anyway. If what they wanted to see was sold out, 28 percent would see a different film while 21 percent would turn around and go home. Avoiding the sticky floor or the spring in the chair that pokes their back, 12 percent of men would rather watch DVDs and videos at home.

A CYBER-GAMER?

One in five men plays video games at home and in the last year, eight percent have done so at a video arcade. Young men (18–24) are big on video wrestling, fighting, and extreme sports, whereas casino, card, arcade, and board video games appeal to 25-to 34-year-old guys. The average gamer is 29, and spends just under three hours a week playing. Two out of every three players are men.

FAVORITES?

Guys like the N64 better than Playstation 1 and much better than Dreamcast. They prefer PS2 by a wide margin over Game Cube and an even greater margin over Xbox. And by an almost three to one margin, Super Nintendo usurps Sega Genesis. Starcraft/Warcraft edges out Age of Empires and Command and Conquer/Red Alert, which dwarf Herzog Zwei and Mech Commander. Only one in four guys has never played any of these games. As for the best turn-based strategy game, guys like Civilization more than Risk and much more than Axis and Allies. And when it comes to fighting and racing games, guys go for Mario Kart much more than Twisted Metal.

A FENCER?

No wonder it's considered elitist. There are only 16,000 competitive fencers in the country, according to the United States Fencing Association. Almost three out of four of them are male. Although foil is most popular of the three weapons, spurred by the recent interest in the Olympics, more newcomers to the sport are interested in saber and épée.

A TENNIS ACE?

The number of guys who wield a racket has dropped precipitously in the last decade but around five million men play tennis, according to the National Sporting Goods Association. Tennis has lost ground as a spectator sport, too, falling behind rodeo, soccer, and even greyhound racing.

BEER LEAGUE BALL?

Some 14.4 million people participated in softball last year, making it the nation's third-most popular team sport, way behind No. 1 basketball (35.4 million) and a tad behind outdoor soccer, according to SGMA International, the trade group of sporting goods makers. Softball participation has softened a lot while soccer has attracted more participants.

HOW ABOUT THE GREAT OUTDOORS?

More than three out of four men (79 percent) love decompressing au naturel. Sixty-two percent get a spiritual lift or adrenaline rush from doing stuff outdoors.

WEAR A HELMET WHEN YOU BIKE OR SKI?

Fugataboutit, say 57 percent of men. Forty percent don't even own any head protector.

GOT A POKER FACE?

Three in every four men have gambled during a recent year. Half (49 percent) bought a lottery ticket and 30 percent went to a casino. Fifteen percent participated in an office pool, 14 percent played a video poker machine, 10 percent bet on pro sports, and six percent bet on college sports. Nine percent played bingo for money. Sixty-one percent played poker or other card games, and 14 percent played them 12 or more times in a year.

GONE SNOWBOARDING? SKIING?

In a recent season, more than seven million folks—about three-fourths of them guys—bought over 16 million lift tickets in hopes of rocketing down a freshly cut super pipe. Nine million went alpine skiing.

PLAYED PAINTBALL?

Splat! In a recent year 10 million guys goggled up to join this battle game at 2,500 sites. Millions more shot each other with compressed-gas guns filled with marble-size paint capsules in backyards and basements.

INTO CYCLING?

Despite Lance Armstrong's dominance of the Tour de France, 93 percent of men have little interest in cycling, says Knowledge Networks. Just two percent are Lance Armstrong wannabes.

EVER BOWL A 300?

Sure, it's a whole lot easier today to bowl an all strikes game (what with better balls and smoother, more level lanes), but fewer than one in 100 men has ever done so. More than 85 percent have bowled however, including 30 percent who've done so in the past year. Fewer than two percent belong to a league. Three percent have gone "Cosmic" or glow-in-the-dark bowling with laser lights, neon, and music to spice things up.

CONSIDER YOURSELF A BLACK BELT IN MEDIA CONSUMPTION?

That has more to do with generation than gender. Young guys tend to fiddle with several influxes at once. More than half (54 percent) carry on simultaneous instant messaging conversations, for example.

IS WINNING WHAT MATTERS?

For 37 percent of men, winning is really all that matters. In sharp contrast, for most women (94 percent) it's more important to be regarded as a good sport and to play the game fairly and honorably.

19

With Eccentricities

WOULD YOU RATHER BE
THOUGHT OF AS SMART OR FUNNY?

Men are a bit more apt than women to hope they come across as smart, but women also hope smart edges out being thought of as a giggle prompter.

GOT AN ADDICTIVE PERSONALITY?

Twenty-eight percent of guys recognize the propensity to addiction in themselves, but 57 percent swear they've got real self-control. Fifteen percent allow themselves free obsessive rein in a few small areas—like gum balls.

CONSIDER YOURSELF A SAMURAI?

Eighteen percent say they're into the self-discipline of a samurai but not the austerity and seven percent embrace the austerity but not the self-discipline. Seventeen percent are wannabes but fall short while 38 percent don't resemble Tom Cruise in any way and don't want to. The rest have no idea what a samurai is.

ARE YOU EXPLOSIVE?

Most guys are slow to anger and eager to avoid it. Only 23 percent erupt when something outrages them—the same number who admit to having hit someone because they were in a heightened state.

EVER THROW A HISSY FIT
BECAUSE OF A ROBOTIC 1-800 CALL?

Even if it is being "recorded for quality assurance purposes" but assuming that it interrupts dinner or something even more intimate, 46 percent of men say they've cursed like banshees at the robot or customer service rep initiating the call. Twelve percent have tried an alternative strategy: dripping honey.

WHAT'S MORE IMPORTANT,
WHOM YOU KNOW OR WHAT YOU KNOW?

More than three out of four men—78 percent—believe that connections are more valuable than expertise.

COMFY WITH AIRPORT X-RAYS THAT
LET SCREENERS SEE WHAT LIES BENEATH?

Two out of three men are cool with the Superman X-ray vision machine that lets security squads see them in their birthday suits. But 30 percent think the threat of terrorism doesn't justify letting some underpaid government employee grope them.

WOULD YOU TAKE A BIRTH CONTROL DRUG?

Forty percent of men reject this flat out while another 40 percent figure that if it's been tested and deemed safe it's worth considering. Another 13 percent are more willing, especially if they thought their partner was preening for a wee one and they weren't ready.

DO YOU KNOW HOW TO DANCE?

More than one in every three guys (35 percent) claim to have two left feet. But 16 percent are would-be Fred Astaires. Half (49 percent) get by on slow dances.

EVER GO BEHIND A TREE?

Women's toilet training and plumbing mandate that they wait in line for a public Porta Potti. Tee-hee. Most men will simply find some shrubbery to do their business.

WHERE OTHER THAN THE JOHN DO YOU PEE?

There's a joke going round to define a schmuck as the guy who gets out of the shower to take a pee. Forty-five percent of men admit they go in the shower, with single ones most apt to relieve themselves there. Some 28 percent even do it in a pool. Men spend an average of 45 seconds using the toilet (v. 79 seconds for women), go on average three times a day, and prefer the toilet paper to be pulled from over the top.

HOW'D YOU FEEL ABOUT
A WOMAN IN CHARGE?

Less than half (46 percent) of men are totally comfortable with the idea of a female president. Many more are comfortable with a female lawyer representing them (71 percent), a female police officer arresting them (69 percent), a female boss berating them (61 percent), or a female doctor inspecting them (55 percent).

DO YOU DO VOLUNTEER WORK?

Whether it's a rural fire department or manning a soup kitchen, more guys are in the act. Fifty-five percent do volunteer work, and among boomers, it's 59 percent. Generation Y men are highly involved but only 49 percent of Generation Xers are in the volunteer trenches.

WHAT DO YOU TRUST?

Not too many of society's institutions: only one in 10 men has faith in corporate leaders and 13 percent believe the stock market is rock solid. Men have more faith in American soldiers (90 percent), military leaders (66 percent), and the American people themselves (61 percent) than in so-called institutions.

WOULD YOU BE A SPERM DONOR?

You go into a basic examining room with dog-eared magazines and a specimen cup, do your business, and come out minutes later with $50 and the sense that you may have helped a childless couple conceive. But for all its appeal—fewer than one in 10 men feel comfortable making a deposit at this bank. Between nine and 10 applicants are turned down. Of those who do contribute, most want to know the outcome of their donation.

DO YOU STAND STILL OR
KEEP MOVING ON AN ESCALATOR?

Sixty-two percent of urbanites keep climbing on an escalator or walking on a moving walkway. The rest let these automated conveyors do the work for them.

WHAT EAR DO YOU PUT YOUR PHONE TO?

For 26 percent of men, the phone almost always nestles on their right ear and for 13 percent the left. The rest either alternate, can't decide, or don't notice.

Likes and Dislikes

Favorite Orchestra Section: Strings with a wide margin over the brass section.

Most Hated Insect: The grub followed by ants, earwigs, brown dog ticks, worms, and fleas respectively.

Preferred Toilet Seat: Sixty-eight percent opt for a conventional seat over a cushioned one, except young men.

Toothbrush: Soft wins 60/40 over a firm bristle toothbrush.

Favorite Ice Cream Flavor: Vanilla.

Favorite Mint Flavor: Peppermint over wintergreen or spearmint.

Favorite Ben & Jerry's Flavor: Chocolate Chip Cookie Dough.

Favorite Smell: The loamy after-rain scent, then the aromas of baking in the oven, newly mowed grass, the interior of a new car, the salt scent of the ocean, and coffee.

Favorite Type of TV Show: Sitcoms, then dramas, documentaries, and sports in that order.

Least Productive Day of the Week: Friday with a slight edge over Thursday.

Most Hated Yankee: George Steinbrenner followed by Derek Jeter.

Favorite Sesame Street Muppet: The Cookie Monster followed by Mr. Snufflupagus, then Grover, then Ernie.

Favorite Dr. Seuss Book: Green Eggs and Ham, followed by *How the Grinch Stole Christmas.*

Favorite Season: Summer.

Worst Karaoke Song: "Achy, Breaky Heart" by Billy Ray Cyrus.

Favorite Body Part of a Bikini-Clad Lass: The legs.

Favorite School Hot Lunch: Pizza followed by tater tot casserole.

Most Hated Slang Word: Metrosexual beats out bling-bling.

Favorite Billionaire: While in 1990 *Spy* gave Donald Trump a measly 16 favorable rating and an unfavorable rating of 40, that magazine is gone and The Donald isn't. His *Apprentice* is an uncontested hit and his parting shot "You're fired" has become a pop-culture idiom. Billionaire businessman and adventurer Sir Richard Branson doesn't catch men the way the comb-over does.

Most Dreaded Form of Torture: Being boiled in oil (beats out being burned at the stake or being drawn and quartered).

IF YOU COULD MOW THE GRASS ANYWHERE, WHERE WOULD YOU CHOOSE?

More men would like to clip the greens at 1600 Pennsylvania Avenue than anywhere else. After the White House they'd ride the mower over the Pebble Beach Golf Course.

VISUALIZE YOURSELF AS THE PROTAGONIST IN FICTION?

Forty percent of men see themselves as the characters they're reading about. Interestingly the same number can get inside the skin of female protagonists as well as male characters.

EVER BEEN SEXUALLY HARASSED?

More than one in three women professes to have been sexually harassed and perhaps surprisingly so have 17 percent of men. Nearly half have been the victim of some crime. Almost a third have been assaulted.

DO YOU WATCH MOVIE CREDITS ALL THE WAY THROUGH?

They must really want to know who the key grips were because 65 percent of guys stay planted in their seats, heedless they'll be stuck in traffic behind those who've bolted for the exits.

WHAT'S YOUR MONOPOLY STRATEGY?

Just 13 percent of men buy the utilities first and four percent try to snap up the green properties. One in four players restricts himself to a few properties and puts hotels everywhere whereas 57 percent let chance dictate: they buy whatever they land on.

WHEN TRAVELING DO YOU LEAVE YOUR LAPTOP AT THE COAT CHECK?

Two out of three guys view checking a laptop a little like Russian roulette. They'll only take the risk at a ritzy club where they are known.

THINK IT'S OKAY FOR WHITES TO CALL BLACK PEOPLE "BRO"?

Half of men think it makes white guys sound dorky. The other half think that if they have a good relationship with that person it establishes a bond.

RATHER BE TRIED BY A JURY OR BY A JUDGE?

Two-thirds of men would rather take their chances with a jury and three out of four think they'll more likely reflect their own views than a judge.

KNOW HOW TO PLAY CHESS?

Just 16 percent of guys don't know the difference between a pawn and a castle.

GET A NEWSPAPER DELIVERED TO YOUR FRONT DOOR?

Forty-one percent get one every day and seven percent only on Sunday. One in four get most of their news online and 13 percent from TV. Sixteen percent read the comics daily.

HOW MANY FILLINGS IN YOUR TEETH?

Remember the old "Look, Mom, no cavities," commercial for Crest? Thirty-two percent of men could have starred in it. At the other extreme, 14 percent have a mouth full of gold with at least 10 fillings.

WANT TO KNOW WHAT HOLLYWOOD CELEBS THINK ABOUT ISSUES?

Two out of three guys couldn't care less and wish these Hollywood handsomes would keep their opinions to themselves. Nineteen percent are interested so they can decide whether to patronize or boycott the stars.

WHEN YOU SPIN ROCKS ON A POND, WHICH WAY DO YOU SPIN 'EM?

Sixty-one percent spin them clockwise; 12 percent, counterclockwise; and the rest either don't know or are ambi-rockorous.

WOULD YOU WANT YOUR KIDS
TO BECOME ASTRONAUTS?

Sixty-two percent think that would be a fine career—certainly better than being a professional athlete despite the enormity of their paycheck. Only 17 percent of guys would gloat about their children turning pro. Assuming that she was gung-ho to enter the Miss America pageant, two out of three dads say they would wholeheartedly support their daughter in this scheme.

HOW DO YOU FEEL ABOUT
THE AUGUSTA NATIONAL GOLF CLUB?

Almost two out of three men (64 percent) think the famed fairway should have the right not to accept women members.

LIKE THE ELECTORAL COLLEGE SYSTEM?

Sure it may not always reflect the popular vote but 56 percent of men favor keeping this institution. One in five believes it's time to reevaluate it.

HOW DO YOU THINK YOU'D DO IN A FISTFIGHT?

Not that you'd ever provoke one, of course, but just say it happened, more than half of men (54 percent) figure they'd do better than the average Joe. More evidence that testosterone equates to positive thinking?

HOW MANY PASSWORDS DO YOU USE FOR ONLINE ACCOUNTS AND REGISTRATIONS?

Forty-two percent have more than they can remember but 19 percent stick to the same one at work and at home. Seventeen percent have two—one for work and one for private.

WHAT'S THE EXPRESSION THAT DRIVES YOU NUTS?

Men find "At the end of the day" to be the most irritating cliché in the English language, trailed only by "at this moment in time," and the constant use of "like," as if it were a form of punctuation. "With all due respect" also packs a tiresome punch.

HOW OFTEN DO YOU WASH YOUR HANDS?

It may not be with Howard Hughes intensity but almost two-thirds of men—63 percent—always wash up before they eat and after they use the loo. Twenty-nine percent scrub after handling money.

FLOWN A KITE RECENTLY?

According to the Census Bureau, 3.5 percent of men flew a kite during the last year. Dads are 58 percent more likely to fly kites than the average American, according to Mediamark Research.

- ► 75 percent have signed the national "do not call" list.
- ► 16 percent sometimes wear their baseball cap on backward.

- ➤ 45 percent of those in the window seat on a plane try to spot their home; 29 percent claim they've succeeded.
- ➤ 31 percent have changed their religion.
- ➤ 50 percent use a nickname.
- ➤ 9 percent stow a weapon bedside to thwart a burglary.
- ➤ 62 percent routinely flip the lights on when they go out.
- ➤ 8 percent usually leave lights on when they leave a room.
- ➤ 10 percent would eat a rat or insect on a reality TV show.
- ➤ Half wake up with the birds. One in four would like to be morning people, if only they could.
- ➤ 18 percent feel embarrassed about passing wind.
- ➤ Less than one percent alert the police when they hear a car alarm.
- ➤ 51 percent grow their own vegetables.
- ➤ 29 percent take something for their nerves.
- ➤ 35 percent would ask their doctor to pull the plug if they were terminally ill.
- ➤ 7 percent think Elvis may still be alive.

HOW DO YOU EXPECT TO DIE?

Probably not in a "catastrophic asteroid strike" (the chance of that is one in 1.96 billion). More men suspect they'll expire in a plane crash than are felled by poor medical care, but according to Wired, the chances of the former are one in 659,779 and of the latter one in 83,720. The chance of perishing in a fire is one in 83,025 and in a car crash, one in 6,585. Thirty-seven percent of men want to be cremated after they die, according to NFO Research.

HOW DO YOU FEEL ABOUT SUICIDE?

Men are slightly more likely than women (29 percent to 22 percent) to believe that suicide is acceptable sometimes, but women are more likely than men to attempt it. However, men commit suicide three times more often than women do. About 15 million people (seven percent of all adults) have tried to take their own life at some point.

DONE "PRE-NEED" ARRANGMENTS?

Eighty-four percent of men believe it's a good idea to prearrange their own funeral but just 22 percent have gotten around to doing so. Of those who have, 92 percent told another person their wishes, 29 percent selected an inscription for their tombstone, and eight percent specified the type of flowers they want surrounding their casket.

THE DISHES: MOUNTAIN OR MOLEHILL?

Some 58 percent get to the dishes immediately after finishing dinner—with women more up to the job than men. One in four wait until later that night to head to the sink while five percent (you know who you are) let the dishes sit for two or more days after a meal.

CARRY ID ON LONG RUNS AND BIKE RIDES?

Experts urge athletes to do so, so medical workers can identify who is suffering from a severe allergic reaction or is an accident victim. But only half of men carry an ID, snap a luggage tag onto their laces, or tape pertinent info to their gear.

DO YOU CONSIDER THE GLASS
HALF FULL OR HALF EMPTY?

While most guys cautiously hedge their bets, saying it rides on the situation, the positive thinkers far outweigh the nay-sayers. Thirty-eight percent describe themselves as optimistic while only five percent believe it's very dark before it goes pitch-black.

STRANDED ON A DESERT ISLAND,
WHAT COULD YOU GIVE UP?

Given a choice among a toothbrush, razor, nail clipper, and soap, far more guys (48 percent) would opt for the soap. A third (35 percent) would choose a toothbrush and 11 percent, a nail clipper. Perhaps spurred by the Tom Hanks look in *Castaway*, just six percent would select a razor. On the mainland, guys would rather keep their cars than their phones or computers.

DO YOU REUSE THE TINFOIL?
SAVE RUBBERBANDS?

Howard Hughes wasn't the only one: 44 percent of guys (led by the rich) reuse tinfoil and 57 percent reuse wrapping paper. Two-thirds collect rubber bands.

WANT TO SUBSTITUTE REAGAN FOR HAMILTON?

Fifty-four percent of men firmly oppose the proposal to swap Alexander Hamilton's portrait on the ten-dollar bill with one of Ronald Reagan.

MAIL IN WARRANTY CARDS? REDEEM AWARDS?

These assurances and perks motivate men to buy but 39 percent of them rarely mail in product warranty cards that come with their new machines. Almost 40 percent have never redeemed rewards earned from retail programs.

GO TO A CHICK FLICK WITH THE HOPE OF GETTING LUCKY?

Three-hankie weepers like *Bridges of Madison County* may be pure sap but more than half of male moviegoers head there with the likelihood of scoring later. Just 22 percent watching multi-explosion buddy action flicks succeed on the love scene, according to research firm Lucozade.

Whatcha Scared Of?

- ➤ 22 percent of men are frightened of snakes.
- ➤ 21 percent are terrified of the dentist's drill.
- ➤ 19 percent of men fear speaking in public.
- ➤ 13 percent of men get queasy at great heights.
- ➤ 11 percent of men fear going to the doctor.
- ➤ 7 percent of men dread flying in a plane.
- ➤ 9 percent of men worry about looking like a sissy.
- ➤ 8 percent fear they'll be shot or badly hurt by a neighbor.
- ➤ 6 percent of men are scared of mice.
- ➤ 4 percent of men are frightened being in a forest.
- ➤ 4 percent of men are scared stiff by spiders and insects.
- ➤ 2 percent of men recoil from thunder and lightning.
- ➤ 2 percent of men shiver at big crowds.
- ➤ 1 percent of men fear being alone at home in the night.
- ➤ 1 percent of men are afraid of dogs.

The National Fire Protection Association says more men consider tornadoes a real risk than fire, hurricanes, earthquakes, floods, and terrorist attacks, but while tornadoes kill about 70 Americans a year, fire kills nearly 4,000.

20

Whaddya Know?

DO YOU KNOW THE INTEREST RATE OF
THE CREDIT CARD YOU USE MOST OFTEN?

You've all got them in your wallets but 34 percent don't know what it's costing them.

MORE A CULTURAL BUFF OR A POLITICAL ONE?

Three out of four guys know the three characters that represent Rice Krispies (Snap, Crackle, and Pop), but just 36 percent could name even one of the Supreme Court justices. Sandra Day O'Connor is highest on the radar screen while John Paul Stevens is the least recalled judge.

GOT THE AMENDMENTS IN
THE BILL OF RIGHTS MEMORIZED?

Forty-five percent say they've got some working knowledge and five percent have the roster down pat.

WHAT DO YOU CONSIDER
THE MOST IMPORTANT INVENTION EVER?

Surprise: it's the toothbrush followed by the car, PC, microwave oven, and cell phone in that order, according to the Massachusetts Institute of Technology.

KNOW ABOUT THE MONA LISA?
HOW ABOUT THE ROSETTA STONE?

While 89 percent of men have studied or know about the Mona Lisa, and 78 percent are familiar with Michelangelo's *Creation of Adam* in the Sistine Chapel, only 39 percent know what the Rosetta Stone is. Even fewer (36 percent) have heard of the Kohinoor Diamond, while fewer than half can identify the Elgin/ Parthenon Marbles. Almost two in three know what the *Venus de Milo* is and half could recognize Botticelli's *Birth of Venus*. Three out of five would know Rodin's *The Thinker* bronze sculpture.

WHAT DO HIROSHIMA
AND NAGASAKI REPRESENT?

Ninety-nine percent are familiar with those Japanese cities and that an atomic bomb was dropped there.

HOW ABOUT WATERGATE?

Almost two out of three men (65 percent) could not describe the basic facts about the episode that toppled the Nixon administration.

KNOW HOW A LIGHTBULB WORKS?

Thirty-seven percent understand it totally and another 27 percent have a good handle on it. Twenty-one percent claim to understand the basic concept whereas 12 percent concede that it's magic.

KNOW WHAT COBRA MEANS?

It's the Consolidated Omnibus Budget Reconciliation Act and it allows ex-employees to continue getting the health coverage they had for 18 months while they secure other insurance.

GOT A GRIP ON YOUR EMPLOYEE BENEFITS?

Only 31 percent of men understand the monetary value of their job benefits—but that's more than the seven percent of women who get it.

RECOGNIZE T. S. ELIOT?
HOW ABOUT WINSTON CHURCHILL?

Sixty percent of men recognize Eliot as a Nobel Prize writer and 71 percent know the other was the prime minister of England during World War II.

SNOOP DOGGY DOGG AND EMERIL LAGASSE?

Three out of four men know who Snoop Doggy Dogg is while 43 percent recognize the chef's name.

KNOW ABOUT RENTAL CAR INSURANCE?

Nearly three out of four men (72 percent) have no idea of the kind of protection provided by supplemental liability waivers; 57 percent don't know about personal accident and effects coverage; and 48 percent are clueless about loss damage waivers. Forty-five percent did not know that rental reimbursement on their personal auto policy covers them if their personal car is in the shop as a result of an accident and they need a replacement car.

THINK YOU'VE GOT GOOD COMMON SENSE?

Although 43 percent of Americans believe they've got uncommon common sense, only seven percent of them actually demonstrate it when given a quiz that measures common sense perception. More men than women think they excel here but women outshone men in the common sense indicator administered by Scott Tissue and Towels. Only four percent of folks think they have less common sense than the average American.

KNOW HOW MUCH UNCOOKED RICE WILL YIELD ONE CUP OF COOKED?

Forty percent of American men know the answer is a ⅓ cup—more than the 28 percent of women who know that.

KNOW HOW A MARGIN CALL WORKS?

Only 14 percent of investors understand that under Federal Reserve rules 25 percent is the level in a margin account below which a brokerage firm may issue a margin call requiring an investor to deposit additional funds or stocks. Nearly two in five investors (39 percent) won't even guess as to the margin call "trigger" level.

KNOW WHERE TRAFALGAR SQUARE IS?

Two out of three men (66 percent) know where to find Trafalgar Square, though fewer than 24 percent have ever visited London.

KNOW WHAT CHAPTER 11 IS?

Almost three in five investors (59 percent) know it describes a company that is seeking protection under bankruptcy law and intends to reorganize itself. Just 23 percent confused Chapter 11 with Chapter 7 proceedings in which a company is seeking protection under bankruptcy law and ceases all operations.

KNOW THE GENERAL MOVEMENT IN THE SKY?

More than half did not know that the Earth goes around the sun in one year. Twenty percent believed the sun orbits the Earth. Another 17 percent thought the Earth goes around the sun once a day.

KNOW WHICH IS BIGGER . . . ATOMS OR ELECTRONS?

Less than half of guys said electrons are smaller than atoms. Twenty percent said electrons were larger than atoms and 37 percent did not know. One out of five believe sound travels faster than light.

Just about half of men . . .

> ➤ don't believe humans evolved from earlier forms of life.
> ➤ believe that rocket launches affect the weather.
> ➤ believe that certain numbers are lucky for some people.

WHAT DID YOU GET IN SCHOOL?

Twenty-four percent of guys got mainly As and 42 percent mostly Bs. Twenty-three percent earned more Cs than anything else and seven percent got Ds and below.

KNOW WHEN AMERICA DECLARED ITSELF FREE?

Sixty-five percent of men knew that the Declaration of Independence was signed in 1776 (v. 55 percent of women).

KNOW WHAT A CREDIT SCORE IS?

Only one in eight men gets that a good credit score will help qualify him for better rates on mortgages, car loans, etc. Four in 10 don't understand that something as simple as paying off a large credit card balance will help improve a credit score.

WHAT WAS YOUR FAVORITE SUBJECT AT SCHOOL?

Surprised that it's history? That topped mathematics by two points and English by six. Eleven percent of students recalled music most fondly while seven percent best liked science. Just six percent most enjoyed art and five percent learning a foreign language.

KNOW WHERE TO GET INSURANCE AGAINST STOCK MARKET LOSSES?

If you do you'd be unique. Just 16 percent of investors know there is no "insurance" for stock market losses. Most people think it's the U.S. Securities and Exchange Commission (33 percent), the Federal Deposit Insurance Corporation (16 percent), and SIPC (16 percent).

REMEMBER YOUR FIRST-GRADE TEACHER?

Just over half of men vaguely remember their first-grade teacher, but almost all have fond memories of their favorite teacher and a vivid detail of how he or she changed their life.

REMEMBER YOUR OWN PHONE NUMBER?

Only 28 percent of people can actually remember their telephone number. Most rely on their mobile phone book instead.

21

Have You Ever . . . ?

SENT BACK A BOTTLE OF WINE?

Drinkers would rather suffer in silence than send back a bottle of "off" wine. Almost three-quarters of men have never rejected a bottle they were unhappy with, probably because of fear of looking stupid or ignorant.

PLAYED CRICKET?

Chances are a lot better if you're not a native American. The English and islanders who grew up standing around for hours waiting to hit a small red ball with a wide, flat bat and run up and down the field as many times as possible have carried their love of the game with them. But fewer than one half of one percent of American men have ever been exposed to it.

HOW ABOUT STRIP POKER?

Four out of five young men turn up their nose at a rite of passage that seems quaint to them. More than half of men of a certain age have done this—as a sequel to spin the bottle.

EVER BEEN BITTEN BY A SNAKE?

Amazingly, slightly more than one in 10 men claim to have felt the perilous fangs and two percent of those say the serpent was poisonous.

HOW ABOUT BY A DOG?

Forty-two percent have at some time in their life been fanged.

CHANGED A DIAPER?

If you're a dad and younger than 80, you have. Men may not do the lioness's share of diaper dousing but they can't escape pitching in.

EVER CRIED AT WORK?

Fewer than one in five men admits he hasn't managed to keep a stiff upper lip on the job whereas three out of every five women admit that at least once they've been sob sisters at work.

WERE YOU EVER A BOY SCOUT?

Forty-eight percent of men were in the Boy Scouts at one time or another, although fewer than five percent ever attained an Eagle badge.

EVER HAD TO USE A FIRE EXTINGUISHER?

Twenty-eight percent of guys have had to aim the big hose at a hot spot.

HAD YOUR CREDIT CARD AUTHORIZATION DENIED?

Thirty percent of men have suffered this indignity at least once. One in five has been denied credit with younger folks likelier than older ones to be rejected.

VOMITED IN PUBLIC?

Sixty-four percent of men have.

HAD DIFFICULTY WITH VOTING EQUIPMENT DURING AN ELECTION?

Four percent of guys have experienced trouble from machines that malfunction or levers that wouldn't go down.

RUN OUT OF MONEY ON VACATION?

That horror has happened to three percent of men.

EVER AS A KID SNUCK OUT
OF THE HOUSE TO GO ON A DATE OR
"BORROW THE CAR" WITHOUT PERMISSION?

Lots of men have snuck out of the house to hang out with the boys but only one in five has circumvented parental authority to go on a date.

BOUGHT SOMETHING FROM
AN INFOMERCIAL?

Eighty-five percent of guys obviously don't believe everything they see on TV. But 15 percent say they've gotten some amazing deals on the tube and that some stuff like the Veg-O-Matic and the Ronco Spray Gun are only sold through infomercials.

BOUGHT A PROGRAM THAT
PROMISED TO MAKE YOU RICH?

Fewer than one in every 100 men has actually subscribed to the bevy of offers for programs that promise to make him rich as Midas. But almost one in 10, at least fleetingly, has contemplated doing so.

BLOWN YOUR COOL AT YOUR KIDS' GAMES?

Seventy-four percent of kids in a *Sports Illustrated* poll claim to have seen adults lose control at their games, mostly in the form of parents yelling at their kids, at coaches, or at officials. Four percent have witnessed outright violence.

EVER MADE A PIECE OF FURNITURE?

Whether with a table saw or hand tool, 73 percent of men say that at some time in their life they've assembled a kit or made some furniture from scratch.

EVER WISH YOU HAD MAGICAL POWERS?

When they were boys, three out of five men (60 percent) wished they had such a supernatural gift.

CALL 900 NUMBERS?

Some 1.2 percent of men say that they do dial them heedless of the toll. But 92 percent claim they've never dialed a 900 number.

CALL 911?

Thirty-six percent of men have summoned emergency help while for four percent of men someone else has done so on their behalf.

LISTEN TO INTERNET RADIO?

While 14 percent of guys often listen and 23 percent do so every now and then, 28 percent of guys have never listened to Internet radio. Another six percent don't even know what it is.

EVER FLASHED?

Fewer than one percent of men has streaked in public.

OPENED YOUR WINDOWS PURPOSELY DURING A CAR WASH?

Two percent of guys say they've opened the windows to see what would happen. (Duh!) Twenty-nine percent have left the antenna up during a car wash and 11 percent failed to shift the car into neutral. Nine percent missed the track for the car's tires and two percent left the sunroof open—accidentally.

BOUNCED A CHECK?

Twenty-seven percent have bounced a check and 42 percent have received an overdraft slip in the mail. Thirty-four percent have had to stop a check at least once.

EVER BAKED A BIRTHDAY CAKE FOR SOMEONE?

Almost half—48 percent—have whipped something up to noticeably delicious results. (Another seven percent have tried—and it bombed.)

EVER SUCKED SOMEONE'S TOES?

Twenty-eight percent of men say they have—or would—and imagine the recipient getting a kick out of it.

EVER BOUGHT YOUR LADY FLOWERS FOR NO OCCASION?

Most men have splurged on these romantic gestures as a guilt offering, but fewer than one in four regularly buys flowers for his sweetie as a sort of insurance policy.

BEEN IN A SUBMARINE?

Discounting the 41 percent who've been in a submarine ride at an amusement park or tourist attraction just under 11 percent have been in a real sub. For most it was in the navy but a few have visited a research sub.

EVER SPEND A MONTH'S SALARY ON SEASON TICKETS?

Splurged, yes. Gone ape, no. Well, not often. Fewer than five percent of guys have even blown a week's pay on special tickets.

EVER BEEN A MEMBER OF A CLASS ACTION SUIT?

Two out of five have participated in a class action suit. Twenty-six percent have benefited including 11 percent who have netted a windfall. Sixteen percent consider these suits rapacious.

PLAN A BUSINESS TRIP AROUND AN AWAY GAME?

Fifty-five percent of guys have. Or if they didn't actually plan the trip they've seized the opportunity when it presented itself.

EVER FAKED IT 'CAUSE YOU COULDN'T HANDLE A BREAKUP THEN?

Eighteen percent of men confess they've pretended because they were secretly no longer into their partner but not ready to deal with the drama of breaking up.

EVER CASH IN YOUR MILES?

Almost 40 percent of men have never redeemed rewards earned for retail programs in which they're enrolled. Yet half say such programs influence which retailers they patronize.

KEPT SOMETHING SECRET FROM YOUR MATE?

How often is ever? Forty-one percent of men (and 42 percent of women) have hushed up something. Interestingly, the sin of omission is more often about what they paid for something than about whom they played with.

SOLD ANYTHING THROUGH AN ONLINE AUCTION SITE?

Lots of men are eBay vets but only 22 percent of them have actually sold merchandise there.

EVER RUN AWAY FROM HOME?

You're not in the majority but you're certainly not alone. Just over one in four of us at some point in our life has broken out.

EVER HAD TROUBLE RAISING THE FLAG?

One in three men over age 40 has significant erectile dysfunction—which is why Viagra and its clones have made their shareholders rich.

EVER HAD "WASH ME" SCRIBBLED ON YOUR CAR?

Twenty-three percent of men shamefacedly admit that "Wash Me" has been scribbled on their car at least once. Some 25 percent have written it on someone else's car.

EVER FEED THE BIRDS AT THE BEACH?

Fifteen percent of guys say they bring or find something to give the feathery flock.

EVER USE A DISPOSABLE CAMERA
LEFT ON TABLES AT WEDDING RECEPTIONS
TO TAKE GROSS SHOTS?

Legend has it that Spike Lee confessed to snapping a picture of his privates to leave for the bride and groom to puzzle over. Seems he was not alone. Forty-two percent of men admit they've spiced up scenes of tossing rice with anonymous body snaps.

EVER HAD A CONDOM BREAK?

Forty-six percent of men had this happen; 19 percent claim they almost had a heart attack discovering it.

EVER PUT IT ON UPSIDE DOWN?

Thirty percent of men initially put them on upside down. Nearly one in three has had a condom slip off during sex.

EVER LOCK YOUR KEYS IN THE CAR?

Ever? How about three or more times, say 26 percent of drivers. Another 51 percent have done so once or twice.

EVER GO TO AN INVESTMENT SEMINAR?

Forty-two percent of men have attended one.

EVER HAD A SEXUALLY TRANSMITTED DISEASE?

More than one in every six men have suffered an STD. One in five has genital herpes.

EVER BEEN THE VICTIM OF A FINANCIAL SCAM?

Just four percent of men have been the victim of a financial scam—or will acknowledge that they have been.

EVER ACCEPTED AN AIRLINE'S OFFER TO GIVE UP YOUR SEAT FOR MONEY?

Twenty-one percent have traded their seat for booty but 17 percent feel their time is more valuable. Forty-four percent have never been asked.

BEEN CONTACTED BY
A COLLECTION AGENT FOR A LATE BILL?

Twenty-three percent have experienced this jolt. Eight percent have missed a debt payment by two months. Forty-one percent have consolidated debt so as to lower interest payments.

GONE TO A TANNING SALON?

Forty-five percent profess they never will, but the rest have either gone or are receptive to going.

CUT UP YOUR CHARGE CARDS
TO AVOID TEMPTATION?

Though it's definitely taking the easy path, 36 percent of men have tried this tactic.

EVER BEEN INSIDE A
WOMEN'S BATHROOM OR LOCKER ROOM?

Thirty-one percent of guys have "accidentally" entered and 14 percent have gone there as part of their job, such as to clean it.

FILED FOR PERSONAL BANKRUPTCY?

Two percent of men have at one point filed for bankruptcy. Seventeen percent have been a creditor in a bankruptcy.

GOTTEN LOCKED OUT OF YOUR HOTEL ROOM?

Almost one in three (31 percent) had to get another key from the front desk.